ARTIA

ANTONÍN DVOŘÁK

The Composer's Life and Work

in Pictures

ANTONÍN DVOŘÁK

The Composer's Life and Work

in Pictures

*

by Antonín Hořejš

1955

ARTIA · PRAGUE

On May Ist, 1954, it was exactly fifty years since the death of Antonín Dvořák. Together with Bedřich Smetana, he is one of the great classics of Czech music, and is rightly considered one of the greatest musicians and artistic figures in the cultural history of humanity. His works come as a climax to the musical compositions of the XIXth century, in which the classical art forms of music were developed on a more popular basis. Antonín Dvořák adhered to this principle in all its implications and in all circumstances, for the simple reason that he came from the people himself. He continued to develop, on a great scale, the democratic tendencies which had illuminated the works of L. van Beethoven, C. M. von Weber and Franz Schubert at the beginning of the century. He was just a simple modest person, who was religious and very sincere. As a musician he was a genius, and this is reflected in his works. For forty years he poured forth his music in a never-ending stream, leaving behind him 120 different compositions. They include 9 symphonies, the most famous being the E minor symphony, "The New World", but his concertos for 'cello, violin and piano are also magnificent. No less remarkable are his chamber music compositions, which number 28, his various symphonic poems and so on. His works are forceful and attractive, but above all they are warmed by human feelings and are always optimistic. His optimism has an eternal quality, a sunlike warmth which people need and appreciate in all corners of the earth. It is for this that he has been and always will be loved.

In comparison to the lives of Beethoven, Chopin and Wagner, Dvořák's life is simple and straightforward. There were no reverses and no great tragedies. There were a number of years of real privation. But for a person who had never been accustomed to wealth this, of course, was not fatal and could not touch the core of his natural optimism. There were, however, moments of sorrow, and they were very genuine, deeply affecting his works. They were caused by the deaths of his beloved children, his parents and his friends. The "Stabat Mater" is just such an example of the depth of his feelings, expressed in music.

Dvořák was a great optimist, he believed in people, in life. His works are, above all, joyful. It seems sometimes as though he must have lived the quiet idyllic life of a contented bourgeois. But it would, however, be a mistake to believe such a thing. So far it has not been possible to unearth all the conflicts through which he had to fight his way or the struggles with which he had to contend during the various stages of his life. After all, it must have been quite a struggle for him to be able to become a composer or even just "a simple Czech musician". It suffices to remind oneself that it is quite a jump from the butcher's chopping-block to the organ school, or to put oneself in the place of an ordinary person who has only had the most elementary schooling and who wants to contend with such highly-educated types of artists as Liszt, Schumann or Wagner. And finally, his world fame did not drop into his lap either. Dvořák had to fight hard for all these things and most of all he had to struggle hard within himself.

In his life there is a period of ten years of which little is known. It is the years 1860—1870. It is known that at that time he was composing hard, that he was strongly affected by all the styles and tendencies of the time, that he kept himself very much to himself, avoiding society, and that he was very shy. It was understandable that a young lad from the country lacked self-confidence as he looked around and came up against an enormous number of ideological and aesthetic opinions with which he was not familiar.

In 1894 he wrote an essay on Fr. Schubert for the Century Illustrated Monthly Magazine. It speaks for all those years of stubborn fighting for knowledge and understanding. His comments, his attitude, his amazing evaluation of the personality and works of Franz Schubert, which he knew in greatest detail, are an indication to what heights he had brought his own education, to what an extent he had come to know and have a vital interest in the various problems that arise in the field of musical composition. And finally, the greatest artists of the time, Brahms, Tchaikovsky, Richter, Bülow, Grieg, R. Strauss, G. Mahler and others, did not just express their dutiful respect to Dvořák. When they met him they immediately formed sincere bonds of friendship, they did not just think of him as a genial musician, but as someone who was humanly and artistically a great and noble personality.

*

Dvořák's life was very straightforward.

He was born on September 8th, 1841, in the little village of Nelahozeves not far from Prague. His father was a butcher, and son Antonín was expected to take on his father's business. He was apprenticed to a butcher at Zlonice but from an early age he showed musical talent. This did not escape the notice of the teachers, J. Spitz in Nelahozeves, and later Josef Toman and Antonín Liehmann, who, like all Czech teachers of that time, were passionate and excellently-trained musicians. They took notice of him, they encouraged his musical talent and they saved him from becoming a butcher and remaining a village musician. They advocated his entrance to the Prague Organ School and he studied there for two years, from 1857 to 1859. It was short preparation for the life of a world-famous master, but it was very important. Dvořák had already had some musical and compositional practice in Liehmann's orchestra in Zlonice. At the Prague Organ School, he came into contact with teachers of some repute, who knew a thing or two and who were able to help such an obvious musical talent as that of the young Antonín Dvořák. Each of them had something to give him. K. Pietsch taught

8

him to love and admire the works of Bach and Handel, J. Foerster to have a genuine attitude to church music, L. J. Zvonař to respect the human voice, and Fr. Blažek and J. Krejčí a conscientious and craftsmanlike consistency in compositional work. He finished his studies and then tried to earn his living. To begin with he became a member of the Komzák café orchestra, which would be divided up and arranged according to the various purposes and places for which it played; later he played for more than 10 years in the orchestra of the Provisional Czech Theatre. He played, but at the same time he was enthusiastically studying and composing. A natural desire for recognition, and an innate desire to compose, to express himself in music, often made him withdraw from life and from people. He had few friends, apart from M. Anger and K. Bendl, who, like himself, also became outstanding musicians. On the other hand he found instruction on every side, all the great classical masters were his teachers and examples. To begin with it was Beethoven, Haydn, Mozart and later Schubert. Then he turned to Liszt, Wagner and Schumann. Works composed under this first creative impulse reflect these jumps and confused strugglings with neo-romantic problems. He staggered from pillar to post, and got almost lost in this cosmopolitan atmosphere. Perhaps he would have lost his way altogether, perhaps he would have completely collapsed if he had not recalled his own background and been drawn along by the national revival movement of the time, by the fervent efforts of the Czech poets, the Czech painters and, above all, by the founder of Czech national music, Bedřich Smetana. It is also necessary to note the fact that it is to the eternal credit of the far-sighted enthusiastic critic, Dr. Ludevít Procházka, that he paid attention to this young groping composer and brought his works to the notice of the public. He thus gave him courage and knowing so well how to guide a young talent in problems of aesthetics and ideology, he explained to Dvořák his function as a composer and the attitude and position he should take regarding Czech national art. At the beginning of the 'seventies, Dvořák began to develop his own critical faculty and underwent a period of serious self-criticism. He destroyed a number of his early works, he once more turned to his own national sources as a basis for composition and finally abandoned the meandering path of cosmopolitanism. The national folk element once more found its way into his music. He had at last realized that he could be nothing else but a composer. He left the Provisional Theatre Orchestra, temporarily he took a post as organist, in order to keep himself and his wife (he had married Anna Čermáková in 1873), and consistently tried to rid himself of every duty that otherwise interfered with his creative work. Not even poverty could dissuade him from this course.

In 1874 two important events occured, affecting the course of Czech music. Bedřich Smetana, who had succeeded in creating a real Czech form of opera and who had to this date produced, amongst other things, a group of dramatic works (The Brandenburgers in Bohemia, The Bartered Bride, Dalibor, The Kiss), and who had been Dvořák's conductor at the Provisional Theatre, was now smitten by a terribly tragic blow — he became deaf. That very same year, Antonín Dvořák was awarded a State Grant of 400 guilders, which was a decisive event in his career and the first stepping stone to world fame. The Beethovenlike tragedy, which had now befallen Smetana, deeply affected every Czech musician at that time, especially such a sensitive person as Dvořák. He worked harder at his composition, as though he now felt that his moral responsibility to the nation had increased manifold. Meanwhile Smetana did not succumb to this treacherous blow of fate. He resigned from his position as conductor, it is true, but on the other hand he threw himself into composition with even greater determination. He produced his most monumental works: My Country, a cycle of 6 symphonic poems, and the great national opera, Libuše. Though Smetana's deafness shocked everyone very greatly, at the same time they were amazed at the perseverance with which he stood up to his fate, at the tenacity, the determination — the magnificent exemplary heroism of this great genius. If other people were astonished at Smetana's heroic attitude when faced with this calamity, imagine how a profound musician, such as Dvořák, who also loved his people, must have felt when he saw this example of unprecedented heroism unfold before his very eyes?

These things have not been written down. Dvořák never expressed his deepest feelings, he never spoke of his inner fights — the only expression of them lies in his works. He reacted to life, to the events that went on around him, by producing works of art. From 1874 on, the curve of his creative activity rose steeply. Therein lay his answer.

Up to now he had been hardworking. He had fought to educate himself and to understand the problems of creative work. Each year, starting with the year 1860, he had produced new works: they included the String Quintet in A minor, Op. 1, in 1861, the String Quartet in A major in 1862, the Symphony in E flat major in 1873 and a number of chamber music works and song cycles. All the influences from which he drew at this time left their mark on the works of this period — and naturally the dilemmas and gropings which accompanied his life were evident also.

But by now he had attained a certain self-confidence and trust in his own powers, in his musicianship, which demanded expression.

The award, in 1874, of the State Grant for which he had applied, gave him the added courage he needed. The awarding commission, which included Johannes Brahms, Eduard Hanslick and J. Herbeck, could not fail to notice the Quartet in D minor which had been submitted to them along with other works. The grant was of both moral and material assistance to Dvořák and such successes always inspired him to further creative endeavours. The first impetus had been the performance of the Hymn "Heirs of the White Mountain", by the "Hlahol" choral society under the direction of Karel Bendl in 1872. It was this success which brought him his first real recognition in his own country and at the same time it bound him to the national tasks which Czech musicians had taken upon themselves.

A much greater success, and one that was of much more influence on his whole future, was that achieved by his "Moravian Duets". He wrote these in 1876 for a married couple, friends of his, the Neffs, and then he sent a copy of them to Brahms for his opinion. Brahms, who had followed Dvořák's development from the time he had first come across his works, recommended them to his publisher, F. Simrock, and advised him to take note of these remarkable compositions. Music circles immediately reacted to their novelty and charm. It is true, Dvořák did not feel this success as far as his purse was concerned, but the publisher realized that he had made a discovery. Events took their course. Simrock's attitude gave Dvořák the assurance that he was on the right road and that he was capable of reaching the greatest heights. Simrock took more and more of his works for his publishing firm, especially when the "Slavonic Dances", which he had indirectly encouraged, won such a sensational success. The success at home, the tremendous success abroad — was like a driving impulse which spurred Dvořák on to further composition, to further mastery, as work after work came under the scrutiny of artists and orchestras the whole world over. He tried his hand at all the various branches of musical composition. He wrote symphonies, chamber music, songs, operas and oratorios. He was gifted with a remarkable facility. His moral ties with Czech music, his world-wide success, which put him on a level with the greatest artists of the time, all gave him courage. His music was original, charming, easily understood, optimistic and very playable and his works were much sought after by all the most famous performers.

His relationship with Brahms soon developed into a close friendship. These two great artists admired and helped each other. Dvořák took on the task of orchestrating the "Hungarian Dances" by Brahms, and Brahms, in his turn, corrected the proofs of Dvořák's works when he was away in America. They had a strong influence on one another. Dvořák made friends on all sides. No sooner had the famous conductor, Hans Richter, come across Dvořák's works than he enthusiastically took it on himself to popularize them in his coming concerts in England. In Wiesbaden, L. Ehlert, on hearing the "Slavonic Dances", prophesied a great future for Dvořák. Josef Joachim and Jean Becker, the founder of the Florentine Quartet, are only two of the great number of friends of his, among performing artists, who included his works in their basic repertoires. And then there was England, which was continuing its proud musical tradition. She considered Dvořák to be a great, dignified figure, worthy to follow in the line of composers, starting with Handel and including Haydn, Beethoven, Weber, Mendelssohn and Gounod, who had written operas, oratorios and orchestral works specifically for England. His first visit there took place in 1884.

Between the years 1874—1884 this great classic writer of Czech music composed more than 70 works. They include three operas (Vanda, 1874, The Peasant a Rogue, 1877, Dimitri, 1882), two symphonies, one in D major and one in D minor, the Violin Concerto in A minor, some overtures, a group of chamber music works and songs, the oratorio "Stabat Mater", "Psalm 149", as well as "Slavonic Dances", the "Slavonic Rhapsodies", "Legends", "Symphonic Variations" and many others.

It was not just a stroke of luck that the London Philharmonic Society and the Royal Albert Hall Choral Society decided to invite Dvořák to come and conduct some of his works himself and commissioned others specifically for England. He had already produced great works which had left behind themselves more than the dazzling trail of a meteorite with its short-lived glory. The world felt that here was music that was securely anchored in the traditions of the finest art, art that embraced all humanity, even though it came from a small country, from the land of a small nation.

Antonín Dvořák made many journeys to England. He was a great favourite there, won tremendous success and was highly honoured. He performed all his great choral works there, including "Heirs of the White Mountain". He was invited to give concerts and take part in the great music festivals of London, Leeds, Birmingham and Worcester. The cantata "The Spectre's Bride" and the oratorio "St. Ludmila" were composed specifically for English festivals, and the Symphony in D minor was written for the London Philharmonic Society.

In the 'eighties of the last century, Dvořák's "Slavonic Dances", "Slavonic Rhapsodies" and symphonies won renown throughout the whole of Europe. The second half of the century was very rich in outstanding musical figures. They were great personalities who, by their very existence and by the greatness of their works, could perhaps have outshone his fascinating rise to fame. There were still Franz Liszt, Johannes Brahms, Anton Bruckner, Edvard Grieg, Saint-Saëns and César Franck. There was also the response awakened by such personalities as Wagner, Berlioz, Schumann and Chopin, who were now a firm component of the musical atmosphere of Europe. And, in addition, in Eastern Europe, there had already appeared such great masters as Balakirev, Borodin, Mussorgsky and Tchaikovsky, who not only made such an impression through their mastery of the art of composition, but also because they introduced a completely unfamiliar new atmosphere into music, new sounds, new rhythms and new types of melodies.

There are basically three features of Dvořák's music which laid the foundations of his world fame: the popular and national character of his compositions and his artistic mastery. These features are not particularly typical only of Dvořák. They are characteristics which appear in many great artists and are the very basis of their artistic personalities. They play a very important part in realistic art. Dvořák's personality was certainly steeped in them, whereas they were lacking in the works of many of his contemporaries, who were not in touch with the people; they mistook cosmopolitanism for nationalism and they replaced real compositional mastery with formal artistry.

In the second half of the 19th century music-lovers began to feel that warmth, sincerity and genuineness of musical expression was disappearing from the works of the composers, that they were losing direct contact with the artists. However all that was lacking in the other composers was to be found in Dvořák's music and this is what lies at the root of his world-wide popularity.

Cosmopolitanism looks upon folk music and national characteristics in art as a drag, which will prevent an artistic work from gaining world-wide response. But Dvořák's career and the success achieved by his works prove that these fears are without foundation. During the period 1860—1870, Dvořák had been bewitched by the personality of Franz Liszt. Under his influence he had groped with the problems of neoromanticism and had nearly lost his way in the maze of cosmopolitanism, only being saved by his own humble origins. And the fact is that the more he moved away from the cosmopolitan attitude, the more spontaneous became the expression of those very folk and national characteristics which in turn won him people's sympathies both at home and abroad. Finally, because his works were so truly national in essence, he was considered as the great representative of Slavonic music. For this reason he was invited to New York to become director of the National Conservatoire, so that, by his example, he could help in the creation of an American national music. It was also the reason why the publisher Simrock seized on his "Moravian Duets" and his "Slavonic Dances", which immediately had such a sensational success throughout the world.

After the uncertain gropings of the years 1860—1870, it was his own natural sincerity that brought him back to the more genuine music of Schubert, Brahms and, above all, Smetana. In their works he found traits that reminded him of his youth. After all, the first twelve years of his life he had spent amongst the people. He had lived amongst the workers who were building railroad-tracks and tunnels, amongst those who went to work in the nearby industrial town of Kladno, and amongst the peasants who had at last rid themselves of the bonds of serfdom and the worst consequences of feudal rule. It was the same in Zlonice, whither he moved in 1853. That was also a small agricultural community, with its merrymaking and gaieties. He had already visited there with the village musicians, when organist Liehmann went along with his band to play for village festivals and solemn occasions. In this way, in dozens of villages, he had seen how the people lived, how there was a universal belief in the unity of the life of people and nature.

Everywhere he went, he came across optimism, that typical characteristic with which Czech people face life and which they instil in others. His country was a beautiful country, its people were brave and gay. And music was a living force in the lives of its people. Hundreds and hundreds of songs mingled in the air. As we know, many became interwoven in the music of Haydn and Mozart, from the times of their journeys through Bohemia, and provide that sense of joyousness which appears in so many of Dvořák's works later on. From his very earliest years he used to make music with the people. During the times when he had played in Liehmann's band, he had had a chance to see what effect music has on people, how much joy it can bring them. It gave him a fervent desire to compose. Just as people invent songs to beautify their lives and to give pleasure, so Dvořák also felt that this was his duty. He inherited and developed this fine characteristic of his people, with its inexhaustible power of melodic and rhythmic invention.

He was always conscious of the popular love of music. Whatever he was writing, and this can be shown in every single work of his, he always thought of people. He always found a means and form of expression that people would understand, so that he could speak to them through his music.

This feeling for the people, which he kept alive by maintaining regular contact with them, is evident throughout his works at all times. It manifested itself, whether he was writing a song to the words of a folk poem or whether he was composing one of his remarkable symphonies or oratorios. And it is this characteristic which, at the time he lived, made his works so attractive. It is this underlying feeling for folk music in an artistic work which makes the work understandable to people the world over and which therefore underlies his universality.

There are two other facts which should be noted in connection with the importance of this feeling for folk music in Dvořák's life and works. First of all there is the way it is reflected in his symphonic works, secondly that it was a powerful protection against decadence. Alongside Brahms, Bruckner and Tchaikovsky, Dvořák is one of the greatest symphonic writers of the second half of the 19th century. His nine symphonies differ fundamentally from all that had been written in this field both before him and during his life-time. Not that he basically tried to alter this great classical form. On the contrary, he felt that architecturally it was the cathedral of all musical art. He understood it and gave it new content and by emphasizing this feeling for folk music, he made an important contribution to the further development and democratisation of the symphony as an art form. He no longer treated it as a "pure music" form, but gave it realistic programmatic content. He, so to speak, made each movement of his symphonies a symphonic poem and filled it with a stream of melody that was based on national folk music. That was how he could create such magnificent works as the D minor and G major symphonies and the sublime E minor "New World" symphony. In his works there are not the slightest signs of any "feudalistic" survivals nor any of the signs of bourgeois decadence which so blatantly manifested themselves in artistic works of the second half of the 19th century. In this connection it is clear that his feeling for folk music proved to be a protection for Dvořák, at a time when, as a result of economic and social crisis, artists, being bewildered and perplexed, often fell a victim to mysticism, abandoned the principle of realism and sought refuge in the chaos of various individualistic ideologies.

Dvořák, a people's artist, one who had grown up with the music of the people, was therefore not affected in the same way by these social and ideological crises. He maintained his sense of direction by keeping in mind above all: the people, the nation, his country and a love for humanity. This indeed saved him. Throughout his life, to the very end, he composed works that were entirely permeated with this feeling for folk music and folk art, whether it was his symphonic poems such as "The Water-Goblin", "The Noon-day Witch", "The Golden Spinning-Wheel", "The Wild Dove" and "The Hero's Song" or his last two operas "Rusalka" and "Armida". And it was this quality which gave his works lasting value, in spite of the period of artistic disintegration, and assured him to this day the position of a classic master in the world history of music.

The national character of his music played a similar role in Dvořák's compositions. He came from a purely Czech surrounding and national traits were therefore innate in him. He began to develop into a fully nationally politically-conscious person at about the age of 25, amongst the circle of patriotic Prague artists, who were the centre of the national revival movement. Up to that time he had had to struggle with these problems alone, both from a technical and from a more general point of view.

The process of his becoming a nationally politically-conscious person ran parallel with the process of his becoming aware of his creative tasks as a composer. Once he had harnessed the elemental force of his musical invention, once he had widened the horizons of his former limited education, he began to understand the political events that were going on in his country, in which all the great Czech artists of the time were taking part.

When he first came to Prague to study, the second glorious stage of the national revival movement was just beginning to unfold. At first the young Dvořák was politically unaware and inactive, not understanding the special character of the position of Czech art within the national revival struggle as a whole.

To start with, he was cut off from this movement, for its influence did not penetrate very much into the sphere of the Komzák orchestra or even into that of the orchestra of the Provisional Theatre, in which he was a viola player. It was only when the composer Smetana returned from Göteborg and became conductor of the orchestra in which Dvořák played, that he finally really got drawn into it. Suddenly Czech musical life received a tremendous impetus towards the creation of an explicit national art of music. The attack was led by Smetana. There developed a lively, militant situation which could not fail to effect every musician. Painting and literature had already produced outstanding national artists and now it was the fight for music. Smetana produced the solution to this fundamental problem of Czech culture. At the end of the 'sixties he wrote three operas, "The Brandenburgers in Bohemia", "The Bartered Bride" and "Dalibor". They set a sure example for future Czech national music and provided a basis for Czech opera.

Naturally these events did not take place without conflict, discussion and struggle and this penetrated into the consciousness of every Czech composer. Antonín Dvořák attended the premières of each of Smetana's operas. He was roused to similar action and to a desire to take part in the creation of a natonal art of music. Still having to contend with the meagre basis of his own education, he nevertheless fought his way to an understanding of the ideological principles of the national struggle. He threw himself into the composition of opera and wrote "Alfred", followed soon after, in 1870, by "The King and the Collier". A feeling for folk music and national traits were becoming more and more evident in his music. And once Bendl had given a public performance of his Hymnus "Heirs of the White Mountain", once he saw that people were interested and he himself began to grasp his own national usefulness, his passion for composition became a veritable avalanche. He had found an aim and meaning for his art, he had made contact with his own people, they accepted his art and needed it. He rejected all his youthful dreams of world citizenship, and the national character of his music developed in all its fullness.

From then on there was no wavering or hesitation. Dvořák concentrated on writing exclusively for the Czech people. Not even the great works which were written to be performed at festivals in England, such as "The Spectre's Bride", "St. Ludmila" and the "Requiem" were of a different style. He found no reason and in no way sought to play down the national character of his music and this was why his works were so acceptable everywhere and were valued as a contribution to the artistic treasures of humanity.

A further feature of his work, his mastery of the art of composition, is profoundly connected with the folk art and with the highly-developed musical culture of his country. Dvořák's country, Bohemia, is a land with an ancient musical culture. Not only the ruling class, but also the common people had claimed their right to make music and had done so from time immemorial. Apart from the folk singers and minstrels, there were the musician-teachers who lived among the people and provided the basis for the formation of music groups, such as choirs and orchestras, among the people themselves. They were remarkable, devoted musicians, who played an important part in the development of the folk art of music in Bohemia. There were many famous musicians among their ranks, who, owing to the unfavourable economic conditions provided by the feudal order, were unable to earn their living at home and left their country to live abroad. They included Jiří and František Benda, J. V. Stamic, J. Mysliveček, A. Rejcha, V. Pichl, Z. Koželuh, Fr. Kramář-Krommer, F. X. Dusík and others.

These musician-teachers can also be thanked for discovering Dvořák. They noticed his remarkable talent and enthusiastically helped him to become a thoroughly sound musician. Fr. Spitz, from Nelahozeves, and J. Toman and Antonín Liehmann, of Zlonice, are reponsible for the fact that Dvořák did not become a butcher. They were representatives of the excellent average musical culture of the country, fine organists and instrumentalists, who had mastered the craft of composition in greatest detail.

Antonín Dvořák went through their school, the school of the simple village musician. It consisted more of practice than theory, but he also learnt something of the pure, systematic art of composition. Both his teachers were composers. Dvořák helped them to create useful, joyful compositions for the people, delighting them with each novelty. In so doing he learnt to respect the human voice and all the basic musical instruments and became aware of the desire of the people to make and hear music and their gratitude if this was made possible.

When he came to the organ school in Prague, he was taught by teachers of a higher grade, men who were nevertheless not unlike his former ones. Fr. Krejčí, F. Blažek, J. Foerster and Zvonař all came from similar backgrounds and all had that same strict regard for perfect and absolutely consistent compositional technique and for clean instrumental playing. Dvořák's compositions, from the time that he spent at the Organ School, are a witness to the high standard of discipline demanded in composition, and an indication of the extent to which he mastered the use of counterpoint and harmonic forms.

What he did not learn from these two grades of schooling, he was able to pick up from the music profession and through his contact with creative musicians. He learnt a great deal from his work in the Komzák and Provisional Theatre orchestras. His great musicianship and practical sense led him to comparisons, evaluations and conclusions, which were important for his own creative work. He took lesson from everything that came to hand, and from everything that he heard. He studied all the available works of the great masters.

He stumbled over problems of aesthetics and philosophy, but by the study of the classics he cultivated a feeling for definite architectural form, through practice he developed a very fine sense for technique in composition and performance, and he evolved certain principles for his own work from his understanding of the relation people have towards music.

The two typical qualities of his, which have been mentioned above, the feeling for folk music and the national character of his music, gradually strengthened his self-confidence, determined the form of his expression and the degree of virtuosity which he achieved in composition.

By the year 1875 he already knew that he must write for his people and that he must link up with the united stream of national culture that was developing.

That was the key to his becoming a master. All other qualities he possessed in unbelievably broad measure. He revelled in musical invention and approached each composition with absolute confidence. In most cases it sufficed for him to make a few rough sketches and then he could immediately write the whole score. Great symphonies, chamber works, whole operas were created in the course of only a few weeks and in one unbroken stream. What compositional bravura! He kept up this high level of achievement from the year 1874 right to the last years of his life. He mastered the various means of expression and created new forms with absolute conviction, amazing people with his instrumentation, with his rich and colourful use of sound and with his expert treatment of the instruments. At the same time he unloosed the springs, both melodically and rhythmically, of his musical inspiration. His harmonic invention and sense of modulation knew no bounds. His ingenuity was astounding. There was creative logic in all that he wrote, a sense of order that bound everything together, that justified everything but which at the same time could be vigorous, witty, gay, ingenious, or sad. This was combined with the fine sense of proportion of a great artist.

Perhaps his greatest compositional achievements were the E minor symphony, "The New World Symphony", and the famous 'cello concerto in B minor. But there are also other great works by Dvořák. They arose from the force of his melodic expression, his technical mastery, and above all, from the passionate and genuine understanding of reality, which dominated his being. The "Stabat Mater" is just such a case, for in this magnificent work he reconciles himself with the cruel reality of the death of his child. The "Moravian Duets" are another example and here the reality is the common Czech people, with its charming gift of poetry and song. Another thing to which he keeps returning and which often raises his compositions to great heights is the beauty of the Czech countryside. He devotes more space to this in his works than to almost anything else, more even than to love lyrics.

Great performers, conductors, choral and orchestral bodies, chamber music ensembles, violinists, pianists and 'cellists, immediately recognized the power his works had of captivating an audience, they could not overlook works that flowed with such unparalleled spontaneity, that were so directly and convincingly effective. Thus his complete mastery of the technique of composition was an important factor in the popularising of his works and in the profound effect which they had on people all over the world.

When Johannes Brahms advised Fritz Simrock to publish some "Moravian Duets" by an unknown Czech composer, Antonín Dvořák, telling him that they would probably sell well, he obviously realized what new strength there was in these compositions. Simrock did not hesitate very long and published the works, for they were so full of human feeling, both in the music and in the poetry. The success was as expected. People found in them an expression of their own feelings. For Dvořák it was a tremendous experience. Through this group of compositions he learnt that the way to people's hearts lay in giving expression to their feelings.

Later, when he wrote the "Slavonic Dances", he really let himself go in this direction. The result was sensational. Simrock knew very well that it could not have been otherwise. He was an experienced publisher who knew the world, an astute business politician, who was interested in works that could be exported. So he contracted Dvořák to write exclusively for him.

That was an important moment.

He made a world-figure of Dvořák and helped him to maintain that position. It also gave Dvořák self-confidence and conviction that he was on the right road.

The fact that Dvořák appeared on the scene when he did, is also an important factor in his whole rise to fame.

During the second half of the century, folk and national characteristics were beginning to disappear from the art of Europe. There were no longer such great personalities as Fr. Schubert and C. M. Weber, and Frederic Chopin, who would have developed them with the same consistency, throughout his life, had died young in 1849. The experiences with Liszt's Hungarian Rhapsodies and Brahm's Hungarian Dances had shown that these were values that were greeted with enthusiasm by both the common people and the bourgeoisie, especially if their origin was the region of Eastern Europe, of which little was known in the west. They were values that were both refreshing and pleasing, being a complete contrast to the gravity and joylessness of the neoromantics and impressionists. It was what the people, what the bourgeoisie, needed and wanted, it was what filled the concert halls and provided the basis of the success of performers and publishers alike.

To whichever work people turned, they felt that Dvořák was a modest person like themselves, who did not try to put himself above other people, who thought like they did, except that he could express his thoughts in music; by depicting his own country, his own life and the life of his people, he was able to talk to mankind throughout the world with complete conviction. He was in fact a realist and nothing could persuade him into being anything else. And just because he was the type of artist who came from the people and depended on them for his inspiration right to the end of his life, he remained strong and sound as an artist and his art became immortal. The world took possession of his works. It did not matter that they were written in Dvořák's mother tongue, what was important was that they were musicianly, clear and understandable, that they were alive, whereas in most cases the results of the beginnings of the disintegration of bourgeois society were already making themselves felt in a deterioration in the musical expression of other great composers. They were also works that made people turn towards the Slavonic regions of Eastern Europe and gave an indication of the forces and values from which the surfeited areas of Western Europe could again draw strength.

The honorary doctorates conferred on Dvořák by the universities of Prague and Cambridge were a fine expression of the attitude which the world had towards him.

But his life was not all glitter and glory. It also had its shady sides. The world only valued and took notice of part of his artistic effort: the orchestral works, the chamber music, instrumental solos, oratorios and songs. The operas, which he tackled with such pertinacity and determination, remained neglected. This was a painful experience. And even though his compositions were performed and served to enrich the repertoires of Czech theatres, they did not have the success accorded to Smetana's operas. The fault however was not only in the librettos. Here his masterly architectural sense, which enabled him to give each instrumental work such solid form, was out of place. The dramatic form was too limited to contain the full scope of Dvořák's melodic line and, on the other hand, the complicated problems of a dramatic work were not to be solved by the most powerful flood of musical invention; Dvořák's one-sided education played a fatal part in this connection, and for this reason much remarkable music in "Alfred", "Vanda" and "The Peasant a Rogue" lies untouched. Only the operas "Dimitri", "The Devil and Kate", "Rusalka" and "The Jacobin" are still treasured.

P. I. Tchaikovsky visited Prague twice in 1888. It was natural that the two artists, who had admired each other at a distance for so long, should wish to meet. These two great people immediately formed a firm friendship. It was specially characteristic of Dvořák's artistic and human nature that his simple straightforward relationship towards people immediately won their confidence and friendship and it was a pity that this friendship came at the end of the great Tchaikovsky's life. Due to his influence, Dvořák then visited Moscow and St. Peterburg. The affinity between them rested, above all, on the fact that they both drew on the fund of folk art and folk music, and as artists they both tried to compose music understandable to ordinary people. Dvořák also always turned with respect to the dramatic works of the great Russian.

Towards the end of the century, when he was in his fifties, Dvořák became a teacher. Dr. Tragy, the president of the Prague Conservatoire, had to do a good deal of persuading, but in the end Dvořák, who was feverishly busy composing work after work, came to realize that it was his duty towards the nation to educate a group of pupils who would carry on the tradition of Czech music and develop it further. He therefore accepted the position of Professor at the Prague Conservatoire; but he soon had to interrupt his work there, owing to an invitation to the United States to become Director of the National Conservatoire of Music in New York. Its founder, Jeanette Thurber, had been entreating him to do this for a long time. Many tempting conditions, material and moral advantages, were the basis for this decision. He spent three years as Director of the National Conservatoire. It was a great honour for just a simple Czech musician. The people of Bohemia were sad to say good-bye to him when he left for New York in 1892, and scarcely anyone believed that he would return. But he did. Life in New York impressed Dvořák to a certain extent. He could also have been well satisfied with the success he had there as an artist and he had the prospect of living there in comfort to the end of his days. The first year, when he had his whole family around him, he even endured staying in America right through the summer holidays, but only because he was able to stay in the town of Spillville amongst his fellow compatriots, because he was able to live among simple people, surrounded by nature and his pigeons.

The second year he felt he must return to Bohemia for the summer, to stay in Vysoká near Příbram, where ten years previously he had bought himself a small sheep-farm and converted it into a charming homestead. He spent two months in the Bohemian country-side amongst his people. The third year he did not renew his American contract. He returned home. He had tried to settle down in America, but he was not one of those who was prepared to desert his country for money. He longed to return and felt it was his duty to live among his own people and work for them. It was very typical of him. One only has to compare the G major symphony, Op. 88, with any single work of the American period, to hear the difference in sound and to recognize the sonorous notes which, in spite of all his efforts to suppress them, echo his nostalgia and secret desires to return home. What he could hide as a person he could not hide as a musician. So that both the F major string quartet and the quintet in E flat major, which he wrote when he was staying in Spillville among his own people, are an expression of endless sweet longing for his country, whose fate was so linked up with his own. He wrote his famous "New World Symphony" in E minor, Op. 95, just half a year after he had gone to live in America. Together with his B minor 'cello concerto, it was the finest work that had ever been written on American soil. It would not have been a truly Dvořákian work, if it had not reflected to some extent impressions, experiences and the various elements of the surroundings in which he lived. He had the very best intention and desire to write something "American". After all, that had been the reason for his being invited to America, in order to help uncover and open the way to the creation of a truly national American music. The symphony is American in so far as Dvořák shows his appreciation of the music of the most fundamental and indigenous section of the American people.

But basically it is a thoroughly Czech work, in the same way that his "Slavonic Dances" are Czech. And even if the "New World Symphony", the F major quartet, the quintet and the violoncello concerto, of 1895, each have their specific qualities which are sometimes considered to be American, there is no question that through them all, Dvořák's longing eyes are cast across the ocean, to faraway Prague, Vysoká and the Czech hills and valleys.

On his return to Prague, he first of all turned to the composition of symphonic poems. Once again he had before him the figure of Liszt, whom he had admired so much in his youth. In 1896 he wrote four symphonic poems to subjects based on ballads from the remarkable collection known as The Bouquet by K. J. Erben. They are masterly works both in form and in composition. "The Hero's Song", which was performed by Gustav Mahler with the Vienna Philharmonic Orchestra, was the last of these symphonic works. In his last years Dvořák devoted all his time to opera. He was drawn to dramatic music, which he enjoyed and found very attractive, as he himself stated. Before leaving for America he had written "The Devil and Kate" and "The Jacobin"; now he chose a fairy-tale theme and wrote the opera "Rusalka". It was the most poetical of all his dramatic works. There followed "Armida", Op. 115, which was his last opera and his last work altogether.

He thus ended his life as an operatic composer and a teacher. He had devoted the last years of his life to the two tasks which he considered to be the most important for the nation: the creation of operatic works, which have the greatest appeal to the broad masses of the people, and the education of a new generation of composers, who would further develop Czech music. He fulfilled both of them.

When he died on May 1st, 1904, he was mourned by the whole Czech people. And the rest of the world was aware that it had lost a great genius.

But his works live on. They echo the songs not only of the Czech, Slovak, Russian, Polish and other Slavonic nations, but also those of the Scottish, Irish, Greek, Latvian, Indian and Negro peoples. He loved and respected men no matter where they came from. This was why people from all parts of the world were drawn to his music. They felt akin to it, because of its infinite warmth, joy and positive attitude to life. They recognized its power of drawing the peoples and nations together, of silencing and driving out hate. This was what determined the fate of his works, that made them immortal and won the respect of the whole world for a modest Czech musician.

ANTONÍN HOŘEJŠ

ANTONÍN DVOŘÁK
The Composer's Life and Work in Pictures

Translated by Jean Layton
Copyright 1955 by Artia Prague
Printed in Czechoslovakia

MACHAUD	GALLUS	CAPRICORNUS	HAYDN	MOZART	WEBER
BEETHOVEN	SCHUBERT	LISZT	WAGNER		TCHAIKOVSKY

*

REJCHA	STAMIC	BENDA	MYSLIVEČEK	DUSÍK
SMETANA	DVOŘÁK	FIBICH	NOVÁK	SUK

A. Dvořák's country, Czechoslovakia — which lies in the centre of Europe — is an ancient land with a highly-developed musical culture. Artists from all over the globe have visited it. The remarkable creative musicianship of its people has presented the world with a number of outstanding musicians and composers. From the common people of this land there arose the great master of music composition of the 19th century — Antonín Dvořák.

Křivoklát Castle

Karlštejn Castle

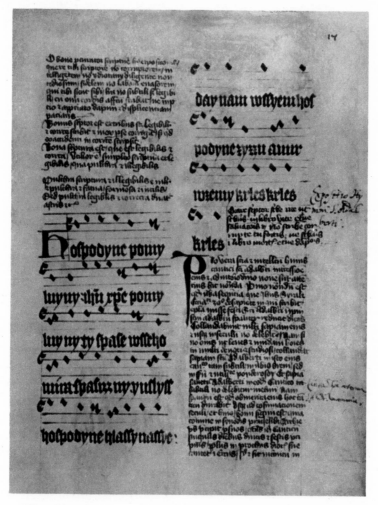

The oldest known manuscript of the song "Lord have mercy upon us" from 1397 — the song is already mentioned as early as 1249

The people expressed their joy, their sorrow, their religious fervour, their fighting spirit and their courage in music and song. It could be heard in the villages, in the numerous castles and manors and in the towns.

J. Willenberger: "The most ancient town of Kouřím"

The gradual from Hradec Králové, 1542

The renovated "Bethlehem Chapel"
— the centre of the Hussite movement in Prague (Model)

M. Aleš: Master John Hus

The Jistebnice Hymnal. Manuscript of the old Hussite song
"Ye warriors of God"

*Dozens of hymnals and other musical documents from the time of the
Hussites and the Hussite movement in the 15th century are witness to
the direct part played by the people in the development of music in that
period.*

The Malostranský Hymnal, Prague (University Library)

Prague as shown in the Schedel Chronicles

Krištof Harant of Polžice — a Czech polyphonist
who was executed in 1621

Šimon Lomnický of Budeč

A. Michna of Otradovice: Holy
Festival Music, 1661

Šamotul Hymnal, 1561

*From the time of J. Trojan Turnovský, J. Rychnovský and Krištof Harant of Polžice, there runs
a line of composers, including Fr. Míča, that leads right up to the beginning of the 19th century.
Even under the most unfavourable political and economic conditions, Czech musical culture was
closely linked in its development with music as it developed in the other parts of Europe.*

Jiří Benda, the creator of the first
musical melodrama

J. V. Stamic, the founder of the
Mannheim school

Josef Mysliveček-Venatorini

*Political, religious and national persecution and the dire economic sit-
uation of the 17th and 18th centuries forced many Czech artists to seek
their living beyond the borders of their country.*

Leopold Koželuh

Vojtěch Jirovec

Anton Rejcha

Fr. Kramář-Krommer

J. V. Stamic, Fr. Benda, Jiří Benda, J. K. Dusík, Jos. Mysliveček–Vena-
torini, J. Vaňhal, Fr. K. Richter, Leop. Koželuh, V. Pichl, V. Jirovec,
Fr. Kramář-Krommer and a number of others played an important part
in the development of the art of music in the most diverse parts of
Europe. They formed a broad Slavonic stream that made its influence
felt on the whole development of world musical culture.

The Stavovské divadlo — the Theatre of the Estates in Prague
— famous for the first performance of Mozart's Don Giovanni
which was given there

V. J. Tomášek

Fr. Škroup, composer of the first Czech opera —
The Tinker (Dráteník) in 1824

The great revolutionary social changes at the turn of the 18th and 19th centuries created conditions for new development in the national life of the Czech and Slovak peoples. There arose a new generation of young composers who felt that the music of Fr. Škroup, rather than the classicism of the faithful V. J. Tomášek, lay more in the interests of the people. In this connection Bedřich Smetana played a decisive role in the evolution of Czech music by creating a national music, and in this he was joined by A. Dvořák, Z. Fibich and the great majority of Czech composers.

Dr. Antonín Dvořák

"...after all, I remain what I have always been — — a simple
Czech musician."

Bohemia, about 1750

Antonín Dvořák, next to Bedřich Smetana the greatest Czech composer, was born in 1841 right in the heart of his native land. He spent the first twelve years of his life in this pleasant, fertile region, drawing strength from its happy surroundings and the people's optimistic attitude to life, which he later learnt to express in his music and bequeathed to the whole world.

The region where Antonín Dvořák was born

Nelahozeves — the birth-place of A. Dvořák, according to an engraving
from the 'forties of the last century

A. Levý: Nelahozeves

Nelahozeves Castle

Nelahozeves Castle

A. Dvořák's family home

*A great son of the Czech people was born in this unpretentious house
in the village below the walls of a 16th century nobleman's castle, at
the time of the break up of the feudal system and the rise of the bourgeoisie to power.*

František Dvořák (1814—1894),
the father of Antonín Dvořák,
and Dvořák's aunt, Josefina Duš-
ková, with whom he lived when
he came to Prague

The room Antonín Dvořák was born in

*His father, František Dvořák, was a modest butcher, inn-keeper and ama-
teur musician; his birth-place was just a simple room in the family house;
the whole life of this genius was marked by its simplicity.*

An entry in the births-registry in Nelahozeves in 1841

The old school which A. Dvořák attended

Kladno, about 1850

The young Dvořák grew up among the peasantry who, up to the year 1848, were weighed down by the burden of feudal labour dues, and among the workers who were building the railway tracks or who worked in the nearby industrial town of Kladno.

Zlonice

"The Great Inn", which was rented by Dvořák's father from the year 1854

Antonín Dvořák lived in the little town of Zlonice from 1853—1857.

The Říp mountain

The ancient town of Slaný

From Zlonice, where one could see the Říp mountain which is shrouded in the legends of the coming of the Czech people to the land, it was only a short distance to Slaný.

The school at Zlonice

The Dietzenhofer church
in Zlonice

The church organ

*Under the guidance of Josef Toman, the choir-master, and Antonín
Liehmann, the organist, A. Dvořák grew up to be a promising musician
both at the school and in the church.*

Josef Toman, the choir-master
in Zlonice

Antonín Liehmann, the organist and
leader of his own village band

These two were instrumental in developing young Dvořák's musical ta-
lent and put him on the way to world fame.

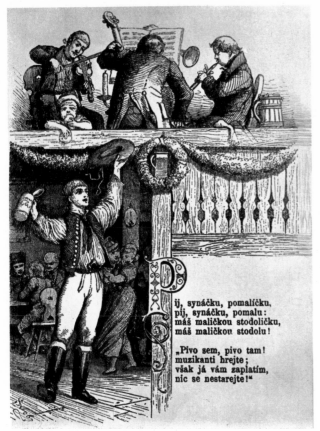

K. Svoboda: A contemporary drawing

Josef Mánes: Lullaby. Drawing from about 1850

Title page to the Rittersberg collection of "Czech National Songs" 1825

Young Dvořák's musical feeling was soundly based on the folk songs and dances which were to be heard in the countryside at that time. All the great Czech artists of that period drew abundantly from that rich source.

P. Maixner: Polka

Title page to the Hilmar collection of polkas

B. Smetana: The Georgina Polka

The new folk dance — the polka — was just becoming very popular when Dvořák was a young man. B. Smetana was also writing polkas and A. Dvořák followed his example.

A polka by Dvořák, written in 1860, during a visit to Zlonice

The Česká Kamenice region

The cathedral at Česká Kamenice

The Choir of the cathedral, where Dvořák used to play

In the Autumn of 1855 A. Dvořák went to Česká Kamenice in order to learn German. There, under the guidance of the choir-master, F. Hancke, his talent was able to mature.

A. Dvořák's apprenticeship papers

From the Český Brod Gradual

In 1856 A. Dvořák began to study the butcher's trade, but his music teachers, Toman and Liehmann, succeeded in persuading his father to let him go and study at the Organ School in Prague. Thus his genius was preserved for a great future.

Prague, the city of a hundred spires — photo by Plicka

A. Dvořák came to Prague in the Autumn of 1857 and lived there for the rest of his life.

V. Morstadt: Prague, the Old Town Square

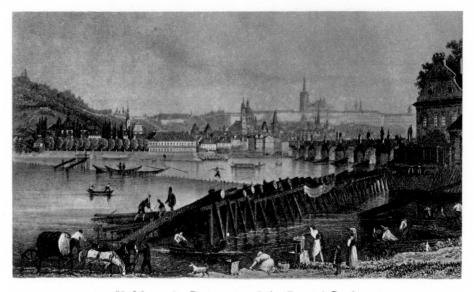

V. Morstadt: Panorama of the Prague Castle

The Franciscan Cloister in Prague, where, in the continuation school, Dvořák completed his education (centre left)

The Organ School in Konvikt, where Antonín Dvořák
studied from the year 1857—1859

Josef Krejčí (1822—1881), director of the School from 1859

Karel Fr. Pietsch (1798—1858), organist, theoretician, and director of the institution

František Blažek, musical theoretician

Josef Foerster, organist and teacher of durch music

Jos. Leop. Zvonař, composer — singing master

These excellent teachers were in charge of Dvořák's talent at the Organ School.

V. Morstadt: The Charles Bridge

The St. Nicholas Church, the work of
K. J. Dietzenhofer (photo Plicka)

*During his first year at the Organ School his way often led over the
Charles Bridge to the St. Nicholas Church where his teacher Pietsch
was the organist.*

Robert Schumann

J. S. Bach

*Robert Schumann and J. S. Bach were two of the pillars on which
Dvořák based his own development as a composer.*

A facsimile of the catalogue of the Prague Organ School from the year 1859, with a note on Dvořák's progress

Ludwig van Beethoven (1770—1827)

W. A. Mozart (1756—1791)

Josef Haydn (1732—1809)

In the early stages of his creative work he adhered to the works of these
three great classical masters and also to that of Franz Schubert.

Franz Schubert (1797—1828),
lith. J. Kriehuber

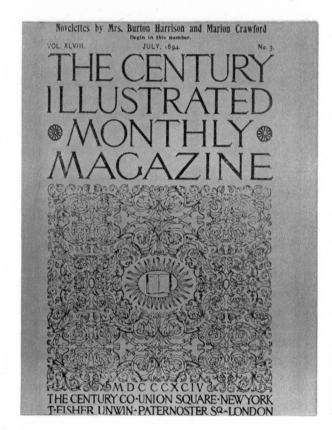

Dvořák's one and only
literary effort was an
essay for "The Century
Illustrated Monthly Ma-
gazine" on Fr. Schubert

*Throughout his life Dvořák maintained a boundless admiration for Franz
Schubert that almost amounted to deep affection.*

Antonín Dvořák (circa 1865)

From 1860 A. Dvořák entered life in earnest and began to participate in the glorious renaissance of Czech culture that was taking place at that time.

Quintet in A minor, Op. I (1861)

*In 1860 he began as a viola player in the Komzák orchestra and from
1862 he became a member of the Provisional Theatre Orchestra. But the
main purpose of his life was to be a composer. In 1861 he produced his
first work — the Quintet in A minor, Op. I.*

Gustav Pfleger-Moravský, author of the
poem "Cypresses"

Karel Bendl, the composer

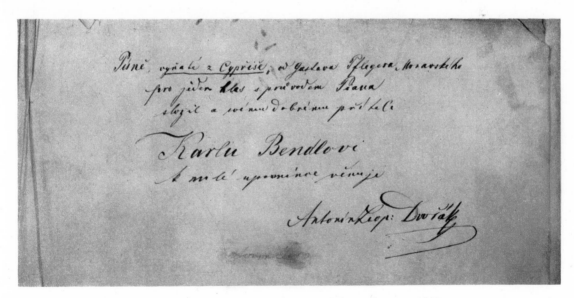

His first Song Cycle "Cypresses" from the year 1865

His first song cycle "Cypresses" was dedicated to his friend Karel Bendl

From the Song Cycle "Cypresses" of the year 1865

The Čermák sisters, one of which — Anna (sitting) — later became his wife. The Song Cycle "Cypresses" was written as an expression of his feelings towards Josefa, who was his first love

Franz Liszt (1811—1886)

Robert Schumann (1810—1856)

Among the personalities whom Dvořák admired were the great neo-romanticists: Franz Liszt, Robert Schumann and Richard Wagner. In the early years he was strongly under their influence.

Third Movement from the Symphony in A minor, known as the "Zlonice Bells", composed between February 16th and March 26th, 1865

In 1865 he composed two symphonies, in A minor and B flat major. His creative talent was developing, he was on the way to becoming a great master.

"Evening Songs", Op. 3, to the words of Vítězslav Hálek, 1876

Richard Wagner

*The remarkable personality of Richard Wagner completely domina-
ted the period of Dvořák's youth.*

Wagner's contacts with Prague were manifold

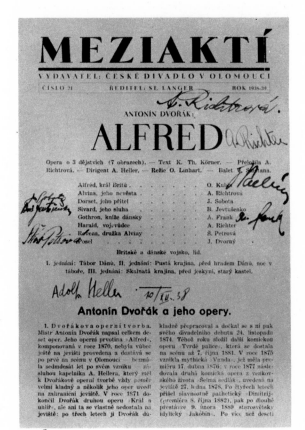

Programme of the First Performance of the opera "Alfred" in Olomouc in 1938

His first operas, "Alfred" (1870) and "King and Collier" (1871) were the works of an enthusiastic "Wagnerian". In his later dramatic works he followed the example of the national operas created by Smetana.

Bedřich Smetana (circa 1860)

B. Smetana (1824—1884) stands to the forefront of all Czech musical life. He was the pioneer and founder of Czech national music. Antonín Dvořák was his immediate successor.

A. Dvořák in the sixties

*In the late sixties Dvořák joined the group of artists who were fighting,
under Smetana's leadership, for a Czech national art.*

Karel Havlíček Borovský, a poet and journalist

K. H. Mácha, the poet

František Palacký — founder of the Czech
science of history

*The creators and consummate artists of Czech literature and art, together
with B. Smetana, raised Czech national art to a European standard.*

Božena Němcová, the writer

Jan Neruda, the poet and journalist

Josef Mánes, the painter

The influence of this famous circle spurred Ant. Dvořák to important artistic endeavours.

The Provisional Theatre (exterior and interior)
built in 1862

From 1862—1873 A. Dvořák was a member of the Provisional Theatre Orchestra. From 1868 he played under Bedřich Smetana. Many of Dvořák's later creative efforts and ideas were inspired by this period.

The orchestra of the Provisional Theatre and its conductor B. Smetana,
in 1870. Third from the top in the second row is the viola player,
A. Dvořák

The foundation stone being solemnly carried to the site of the National Theatre

The "Father of the Nation", the historian František Palacký, at the ceremonial laying of the foundation stone

The laying of the foundation stone of the dignified new building of the National Theatre in 1868 was a great national celebration. The theatre was built by means of money collected from the whole nation.

B. Smetana, about 1868

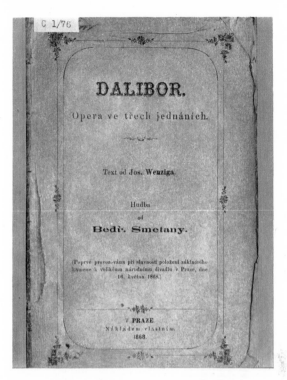

First edition of the piano score
of the opera "Dalibor"

Part of the score of "The Bartered Bride"
by Smetana

*It was at this time that B. Smetana finally succeeded in solving the
problem of Czech national opera in his works: "The Brandenburgers
in Bohemia" 1863, "The Bartered Bride" 1866, "Dalibor" 1868.*

Karel Šebor

Vojtěch Hřímalý

Josef Richard Rozkošný

Vilém Blodek

Other Czech composers supported Smetana's endeavours. The fight for Czech national art developed on a broad scale.

Ludevít Procházka, critic, composer,
conductor and organiser of Czech
musical life

Professor Otokar Hostinský, aesthetician
and founder of Czech musicology

Dr. Ludevít Procházka and Dr. O. Hostinský, young militant critics,
introduced Dvořák to the great stream of Czech music when he was
still a young man.

Programmes of musical evenings at which the Prague public were able to become acquainted with contemporary Czech compositions

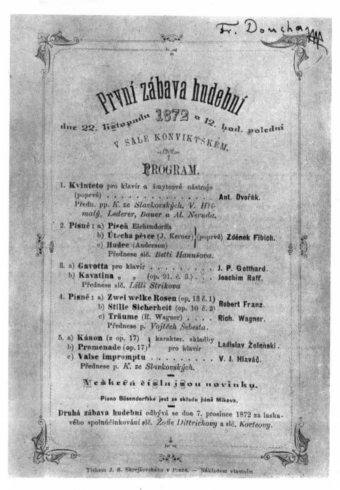

Works by Dvořák were performed at two of such musical evenings organised by Procházka. It was his first acquaintance with the public and it had a marked effect on the further creative activity of the young composer.

E. Chvála

Zdeněk Fibich

V. J. Novotný

Gifted and enthusiastic critics, including among others Z. Fibich, a classic
master of Czech music, prophesied a great future for Dvořák.

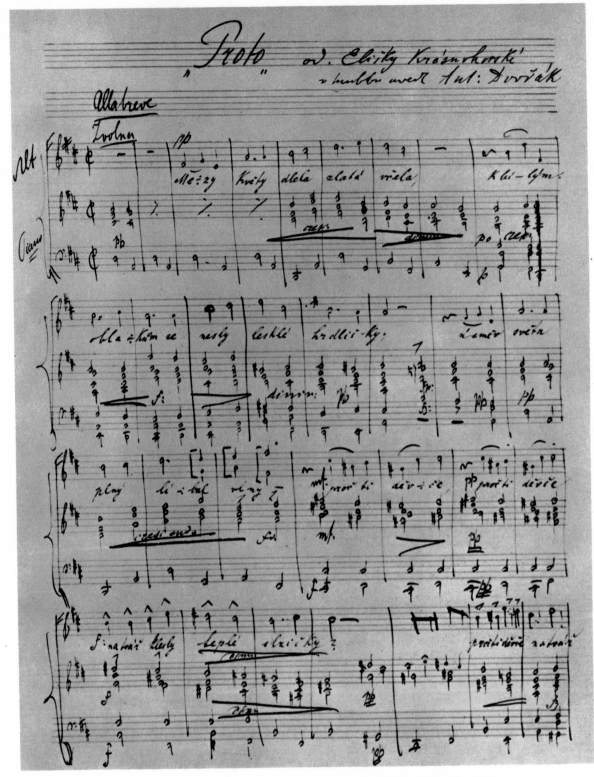

"Because". One of Dvořák's songs to a text by Eliška Krásnohorská

Eliška Krásnohorská, B. Smetana's librettist

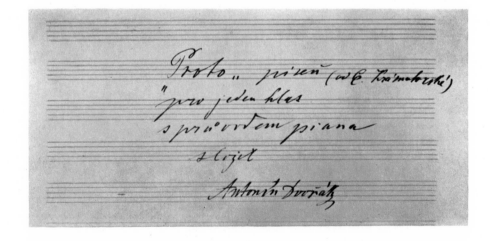

Dvořák began to create new Czech music. His works emphasized national and folk elements. He turned to the works of the Czech poets: Eliška Krásnohorská, K. J. Erben, Vítězslav Hálek etc.

Karel Bendl, about 1880

Karel Bendl (1838—1897), the author of several operas, numerous songs
and choruses, was a devoted friend of Dvořák's from the Organ School.

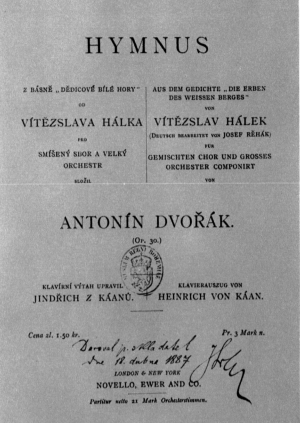

The piano score of the "Hymnus"

Programme of the First Performance of Dvořák's hymnus "Heirs of the White Mountain"

Karel Bendl, with the Hlahol choir, gave the first performance of the "Hymnus", which was considered a great success for Dvořák and this had a decisive influence on his position in Czech music.

In 1873 A. Dvořák married Anna Čermáková

The house "Na Rybníčku", No. 14

The end of the opera "The Pig-headed Ones"

In his first home "Na Rybníčku" (1874—1877) Dvořák lived through hard times and also witnessed the death of two of his children. However he also produced a number of masterly works beginning with the Symphony in D minor.

The St. Ethelbert Church in Prague

*In 1873 A. Dvořák left the Provisional Theatre orchestra and took the
post of organist in the St. Ethelbert church. With this job he had time
for creative work.*

Scherzo from the D minor Symphony, composed in 1874

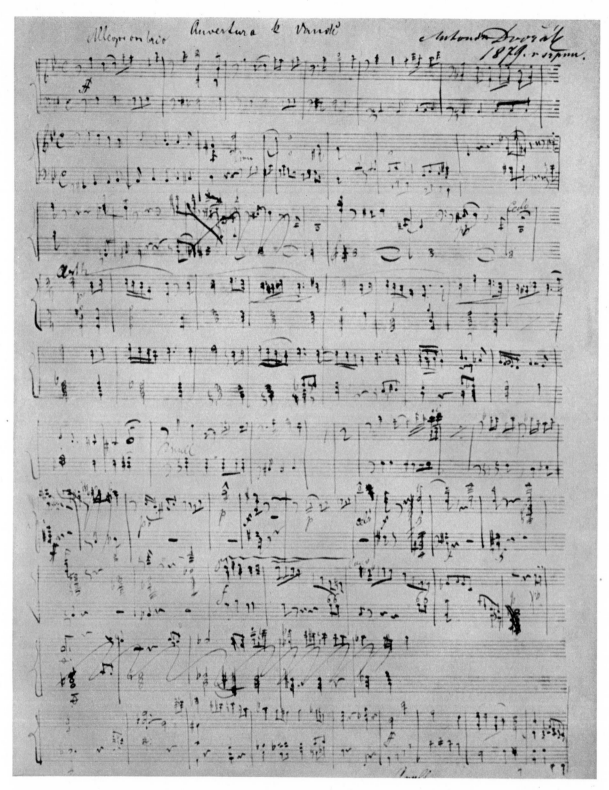

Overture to the opera "Vanda"

Under the influence of Smetana's works, between 1874—1877, Dvořák reworked the score of "The King and The Collier" and created new operas, "The Pig-headed Ones" in 1874, "Vanda" in 1875, "The Peasant a Rogue" in 1877.

Programme of the first performance of the opera "The Peasant a Rogue" in Prague

The theatre in Dresden, where the opera "The Peasant a Rogue" received its first performance outside the country

Followings its first performance in Prague in 1878, the opera, "The Peasant a Rogue", was performed in Dresden in 1882, in Hamburg in 1883, in Vienna in 1885.

String Quartet in E major, Op. 27

In the period 1873—1877 he wrote 6 string quartets, a piano trio in B flat major, a string quintet in D major and an octet which has been lost.

Lad. Dolanský

J. Srb-Debrnov

V. Zelený

Conscientious critics and theoreticians, who advocated Dvořák's works and influenced the direction of his creative activity.

From the score of the "Stabat Mater"

The famous "Stabat Mater", a composition for solo quartet, chorus and orchestra, Op. 58, is an expression of his personal sorrow over the loss of his children.

From the score of the "Stabat Mater"

From the "Evening Songs", Op. 31

After the great creative effort of the "Stabat Mater", A. Dvořák turned to the charming collection of lyrical poems by Vítězslav Hálek: "Evening Songs".

Vítězslav Hálek was also the author of the poem, "Heirs of the White Mountain" to which Dvořák composed his "Hymnus", Op. 30

Manuscript of the song "I dreamt that you had died"

He arranged some of the "Evening Songs" with orchestral accompaniment for his friend, the singer Josef Lev.

First Czech edition of the
"Moravian Duets"

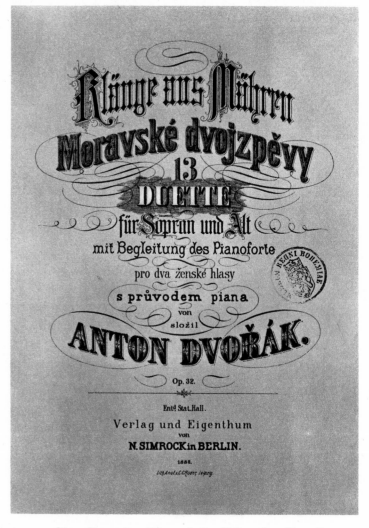

First Simrock edition of the "Moravian Duets"

Dvořák wrote the "Duets" Op. 20, 29, 31, for a married couple called Neff, who were friends of his. He set them to words from Moravian folk poetry. On Brahm's recommendation they were published by the firm of Simrock in Berlin.

Dvořák's manuscript of the 14th duet, "Omens"

From the years 1874—1877, A. Dvořák applied for a state stipendium.
The commission that awarded the grants consisted, among others, of Ed.
Hanslick, J. Herbeck and Johannes Brahms. The latter was attracted by
the "Duets" and forwarded them to Fr. Simrock, drawing his attention
to Dvořák.

Hugo Boettinger: Antonín Dvořák

*In gratitude Dvořák dedicated his String Quartet in D minor to Brahms
for the interest he had taken in him.*

Johannes Brahms

A great and noble friendship grew up between the two masters, who were two of the greatest composers of music during the second half of the 19th century.

A letter from Brahms to Dvořák, 1879

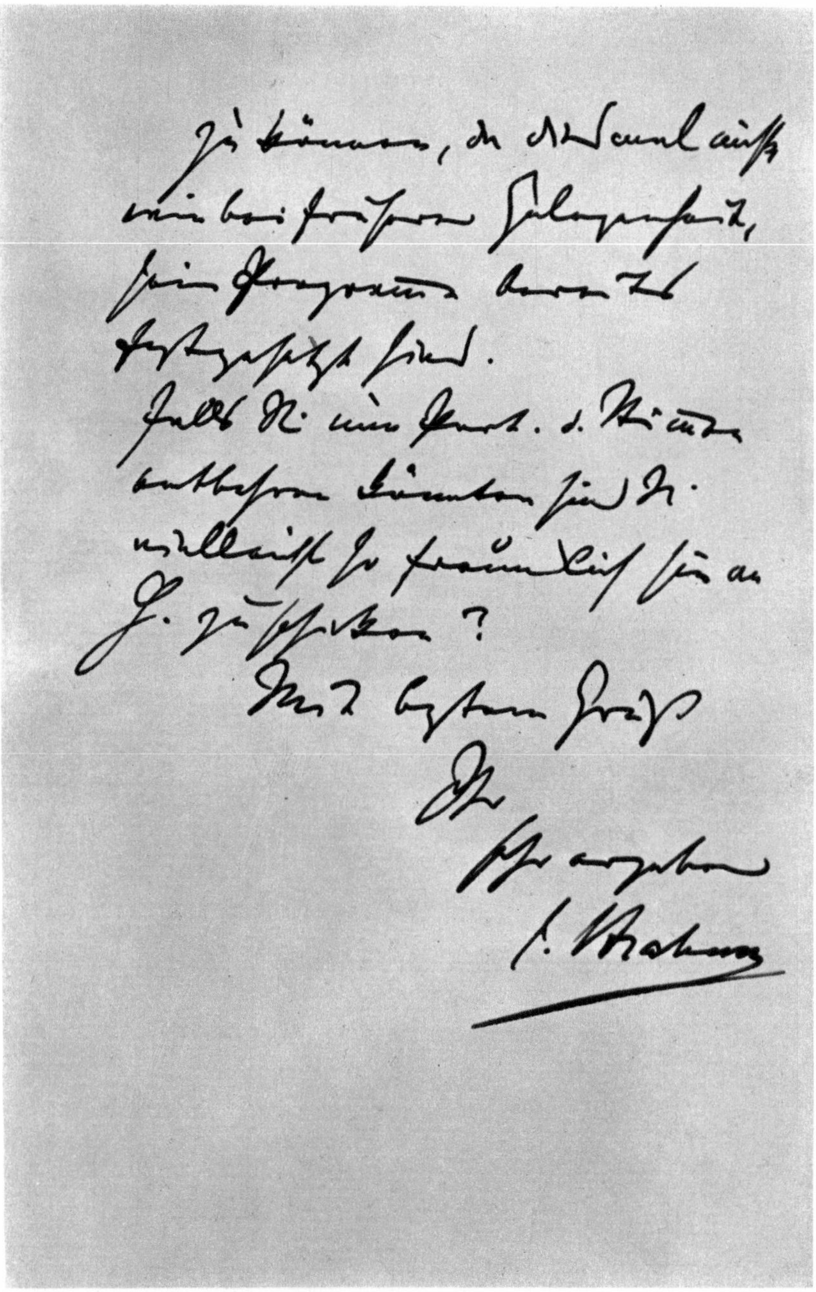

zu können, da ... auch
... bei ... Gelegenheit,
... ...
...

Falls ... ...
... ...
vielleicht so freundlich ... an
... zu schicken?

Mit bestem Gruß

Ihr
ergebener
J. Brahms

Johannes Brahms

"Brahms at the piano" — a drawing
by W. von Bechrath

*They maintained the friendship right up to the end of Brahms' life and
had a strong influence on each other. Dvořák often visited Brahms and
was present at his funeral.*

Orchestral arrangement of the "17th Hungarian Dance" by J. Brahms

Dr. O. Böhler: Brahms
on his way to the "Red
Hedgehog"

*A. Dvořák arranged Brahms's Hungarian Dances for orchestra. On the
other hand, while Dvořák was in America, Brahms corrected the proofs
of his New World Symphony.*

Dvořák's arrangement of Brahms's 18th "Hungarian Dance"

A contemporary caricature —
Hanslick and Brahms

Fritz Simrock

Karlovy Vary (Carlsbad)

Fritz Simrock played an important part in Dvořák's life, as his publisher. At an early stage he realized his greatness. They had frequent meetings at Karlovy Vary.

 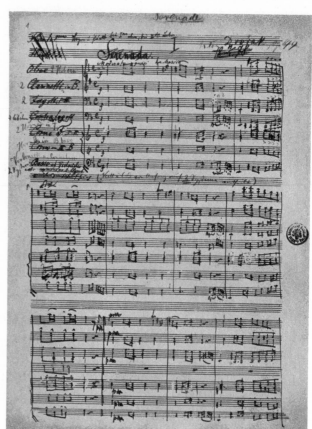

Serenade in D minor for wind instruments, Op. 44, dedicated to L. Ehlert

He dedicated his D minor "Serenade", Op. 44, to L. Ehlert of Wiesbaden, who had written enthusiastically about his "Slavonic Dances" and thus roused people's interest in his works.

From 1877 till his death he lived in
No. 14, Žitná ulice

The Charles Square with the St. Ignace
church (in the foreground) was the ob-
ject of his daily walks

Prague Stations in Dvořák's time.

The kinds of locomotives that used
to arrive at the stations

*Dvořák used to visit the station everyday. He admired and knew all the
engines and the engine-drivers. This passion of his also manifested itself
during his stay in America.*

"Slavonic Rhapsody", Op. 45, No. 3

The works of the great Russian classical masters and his own interest in Slavism led him to seek inspiration first in Czech songs and dances and later in the very sources of Slavonic folk music.

"Slavonic Dance" No. I, piano duet

The "Slavonic Dances" brought Dvořák world fame. Originally written for the piano as a duet for four hands, as in the case of the first series, Op. 46 of 1876, which were followed by the second series, Op. 72 in 1886.

"Slavonic Dance" No. 4, arranged for orchestra

In 1879 Simrock published the "Slavonic Dances" as arranged for orchestra. The success of these prepared the way for other compositions.

"Slavonic Dance" No. 7, arranged for orchestra

The "Slavonic Dances" and the "Slavonic Rhapsodies" were a powerful expression of the national character which Dvořák emphasized so much in his later works.

Antonín Dvořák 1879

Dvořák's works were often to be heard in the concert hall on the Sophie Island

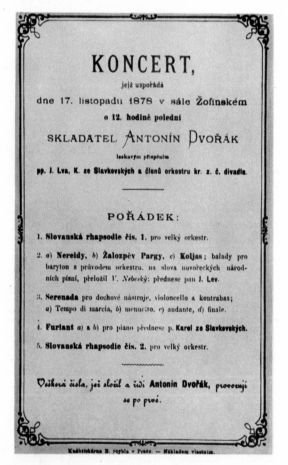

There were concerts of Dvořák's works which he conducted himself

By the end of the seventies, A. Dvořák's works were very often to be heard at Prague concerts and gradually his works were becoming known in the world abroad.

Excerpt from Op. 27 "Five Male Voice Choruses"

"Two Male Voice Choruses"; arrangements of Irish national songs

*The hundreds of Czech choral societies inspired Dvořák to write choral
music.*

The ancient town of Turnov

The Turnov region — a contemporary drawing

A. Dvořák passed many happy times in the Turnov region, where he used to spend the summer months between the years 1878—96. He was happiest amongst the common people and amid the beauties of nature.

Sychrov Castle

Ještěd, in the district of Světlá, the scene of the novels of the writer
Karolina Světlá

*Half-way between Turnov and the Ještěd mountain lies the Rohan castle
of Sychrov. Dvořák had a good friend living there, the well-known
singer and enthusiastic Czech musician A. Göbl.*

The Brittany tower of the Sychrov castle

Alois Göbl, Dvořák's friend who lived at Sychrov

The Sychrov castle park, the scene of the annual Dvořák festival

The Trio, Ferd. Lachner, Ant. Dvořák, Hanuš Wihan, on the occasion of a concert visit
to Turnov, in 1892, also visited Sychrov.

It was in Sychrov, in 1879, that A. Dvořák began writing his famous violin concerto in A minor, Op. 53, which he dedicated to Josef Joachim.

Josef Joachim

Josef Joachim was an enthusiastic admirer of A. Dvořák and a keen propagator of his works, both as a famous soloist and as the leader of the Joachim quartet.

The beginnings of the IInd and IIIrd movements of the violin concerto
in A minor, Op. 53

Waltz No. 1, written in 1880   "From the Bohemian Forest"

"Waltzes" and the cycle "From the Bohemian Forest" were an expression of the period when publishers fully exploited Dvořák's popularity throughout the world. Into this period also belong the "Gypsy Melodies" Op. 55, a cycle of poems to words by A. Heyduk.

Excerpt from the "Gypsy Melodies", Op. 55

Professor Dr. Josef Zubatý,
Dvořák's collaborator

Adolf Heyduk, a Czech poet, to
whose lyrics Dvořák often turned

Adolf Čech

K. Knittl

Leoš Janáček

Apart from B. Smetana, L. Procházka and Slánský, the first successful propagators of Dvořák's works in the early years were Adolf Čech, K. Knittl and Leoš Janáček, a good friend of Dvořák's.

Sonata for Violin and Piano, Op. 57

Mořic Anger

*Mořic Anger, the conductor of the Provisional Theatre, gave performan-
ces of Dvořák's orchestral and operatic works throughout his life. When
Dvořák came to Prague they lived together. Anger prevented the A minor
symphony from being destroyed,*

J. Mánes: The banner of the Hlahol Choral Society

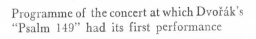

Programme of the concert at which Dvořák's "Psalm 149" had its first performance

The first home of the "Hlahol" choir

The "Hlahol" choral society was an enthusiastic propagator of Dvořák's works. The high standard of performance attained by the choir encouraged Dvořák to write numerous vocal works.

"Legends", Op. 59, later arranged for orchestra, was dedicated to Eduard Hanslick

Professor Ed. Hanslick

E. Hanslick, the Vienna critic and friend of Brahms, took a very positive attitude to Dvořák and his works.

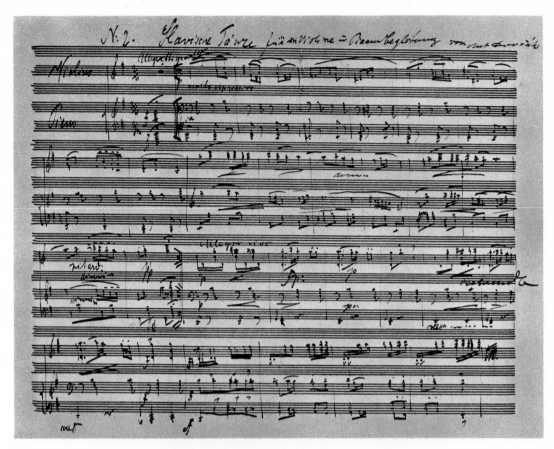

"Slavonic Dances", Dvořák's arrangement for Violin and Piano

Dvořák's passport

Hans Richter

R. Wagner's great friend, the famous conductor of the Vienna Philharmonic Orchestra, became a devoted admirer and friend of Dvořák's. He introduced Dvořák's works at many of his concerts.

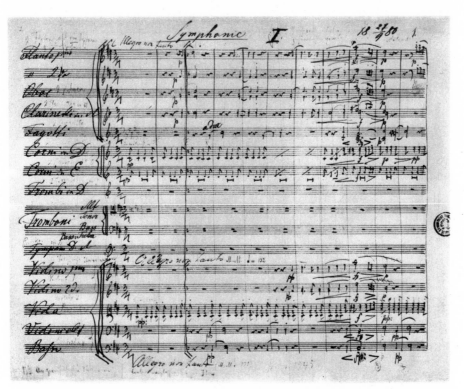

The D major Symphony Op. 60, dedicated to Hans Richter

Hans Richter introduced Dvořák's works into England. As early as 1880 he performed the IIIrd Slavonic Rhapsody there, and in 1882 the D major symphony.

17. May. 1887.

Lieber verehrter Freund!

[handwritten letter in German cursive]

Hans Richter

The numerous enthusiastic letters from Richter to Dvořák are a documentary proof

24. Jänner. 1902.

THE FIRS,
BOWDON,
CHESHIRE.

Verehrter lieber Freund!

Nach dem grossen Genuss, den uns Allen
gestern Ihre D-dur Symphonie bereitete
drängt es mich, Ihnen einige Zeilen zu schreiben.
Ich weiß nicht, ob Sie benachrichtigt sind,
daß wir in Manchester und den Städten, die
ich mit meinem Orchester bereise, sehr fleißig
mit Ihren Compositionen am Werke sind;
Ihr Name gehört zu den häufigst vor-
kommenden auf meinen Programmen. Ich
schreibe Ihnen dieses, weil ich annehme,
daß es Ihnen Freude macht; nicht aber,
um dafür von Ihnen Lob zu erwerben. Es ist

meine Pflicht, für gute und schöne Werke
mit all' meiner Begabung einzutreten und
sie zu fördern; und Sie machen mir diese
Pflichterfüllung so leicht und erfreulich.
Also kein Wort des Dankes, sonst schicke
ich Ihnen keine Programme mehr. — Nun
bitte ich Sie aber, eine Sache fest stellen zu
wollen, das ist die Nummer der Symphonie.
Ich weiß nicht, ob die Angabe des Kritikers —
ich lege die Kritik deren in das Programmbuch —
ganz richtig, glaube mich aber richtig zu erinnern,
wenn ich annehme, daß vor der D-dur Symphonie
schon eine erste componirt war. Wie groß
war also mein Erstaunen, als ich auf dem
Titelblatte der D-moll Symphonie die N° 2

of the fact that by the eighties Dvořák was already a world famous composer

The Vienna Philharmonic — H. Richter in the centre

Dvořák wrote charming incidental music to Šamberg's play, "Josef Kajetán Tyl". The Overture under the title, "My Country", is an excellent orchestral work

Karel Kovařovic

K. Kovařovic gave a new production of "Dimitri" in 1906.

Scene from "Dimitri"

The New Czech Theatre (1876—1886) behind the Žitná Gate

A poster for the First Performance
of "Dimitri"

*The opera "Dimitri", 1882, belongs to the group of works of his so-called
"Slavonic period".*

Hans von Bülow

"The most important composer for me, apart from Brahms, is Dvořák"
(H. v. Bülow).

The famous German conductor and pianist, Hans von Bülow, met Dvořák as early as 1859, soon ofter he first came to Prague. He became an enthusiastic protagonist of Dvořák's works as soon as he got to know the Hussite Overture. Bülow was a frequent visitor to Prague.

"The Hussite Overture" Op. 67, written for the opening of the National Theatre in 1883

The "Joachim Quartet", with J. Joachim as leader

The "Florentine Quartet": Jean Becker, E. Masi,
L. Chiostri, L. Hegyesi

*A. Dvořák greatly enriched the repertoire of the two famous ensembles,
the Florentine Quartet and the Joachim Quartet which, especially in the
'eighties, helped to spread Dvořák's fame throughout Europe.*

Prof. Hanuš Trneček   Prof. Josef Jiránek   Prof. A. Bennewitz

Pavel Křížkovský,
the composer

Josef Lev, the singer

The Chamber Music Ensemble: Lachner, Rauscher, Neruda and
Krehan, protagonists of new Czech chamber music

*More and more Czech musicians were beginning to play the works of
Antonín Dvořák.*

Antonín Dvořák 1885

In 1884, on the invitation of the Philharmonic Society and the Royal
Albert Hall Choral Society, Dvořák went to England in order to conduct
some of his own works there. The ten years of contact with this land
of great musical culture were marked by tremendous successes, great
honours and the enthusiasm and love shown to him by the British people.

The Crystal Palace, Sydenham

In 1883 Josef Barnby gave the first performance in London of the "Stabat Mater", which led to the invitation to visit England. The performance of the "Slavonic Dances" also called attention to Dvořák as a composer.

The Royal Albert Hall, London

A. Dvořák with his wife in London
in 1886

The composer Jindřich Kaán accompanied A. Dvořák on his first visit
to London

*The Crystal Palace and the Royal Albert Hall, London, were the scenes
of Dvořák's successes.*

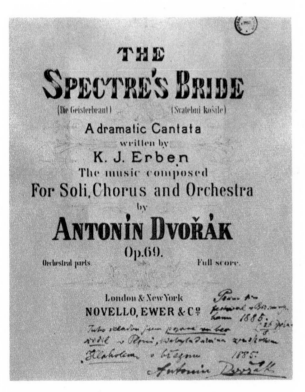

The title page of the score of the D minor Symphony

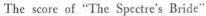

The score of "The Spectre's Bride"

K. I. Farský: K. J. Erben (Lithograph)

*In 1884 he composed a cantata, to the words of the ballad "The Spectre's
Bride" by the Czech poet K. J. Erben, for the Birmingham Music Festival.*

Hochgeehrter Meister!

Eine Widmung von Ihnen — dem nächst Brahms gottbegnadetsten Tondichter der Gegenwart — das ist eine höhere Auszeichnung, als irgend welcher Großkreuz seitens irgend welches Fürsten. Mit meinem herzlichsten Danke nehme ich diese Ehre an.

Ihr in aufrichtigster Hochachtung
ergebener Bewunderer

Hans v. Bülow

Hamburg 25 Nov. 1887.

Hans v. Bülow to Dvořák

Henry Littleton

Westwood House, Sydenham

Henry Littleton, the owner of the firm Novello, Ewer and Company, was a real admirer and friend of Dvořák's. Dvořák lived at Westwood House during his stay in London.

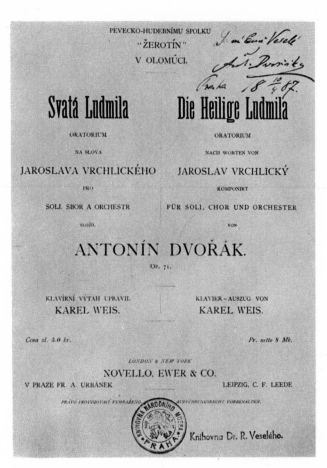

Piano score of the oratorio "St. Ludmila"

Max Švabinský: Jaroslav Vrchlický

Leeds Town Hall

*Dvořák's national oratorio "St. Ludmila" was given a festive first perform-
ance in Leeds on October 15th, 1886. The text is by the great Czech
poet Jaroslav Vrchlický.*

Manuscript of the score of the first part of the oratorio "St. Ludmila"

A letter to Dr. Mandyczewsky in Vienna in which he describes the reception accorded his oratorio "St. Ludmila". Later, along with Dr. Mandyczewsky, in place of Brahms, he became a member of the state commission which awarded the musical stipends

1887. – Ich ogin ... mit auch dem
...

Die ersten 4 ... waren
unter meiner Leitung, die hinteren
2 dirigirte Herr Regensburgmstr.
Moritz Anger.

Im nächsten Jahr wurde das
Werk in Olmütz, von dem
slav. Gesangsverein "Žerotín"
und zwar zweimal, in beiden
mit wiederholt. Den hier
Kremsier Anstalt in Mähren,
dem Gesangverein "Moravan."
In Olmütz hat sich der hochwürdige
Vikar Pater H. Geisler, so
wie in Kremsier Herr
Dr. Emil Kozánek ...
... für die Aufführung
meines Werkes verdient.

... in Amerika wollte Ludovic ...
Aufführung, aber ich ...
... der Herrn der Stadt
... geblieben!
... ist die ganze Wanderung.
meines Werkes in der musikalische
Welt – möge es ihm auch
in Wien ... eilergehen ...
Das Stück spielte mehr als 3 Stunden.
Ich habe jetzt Herrn Verger ersucht,
das Stück mit Auszügen zu geben.
was ... großtheils des
Werkes ist. Jetzt 100 ...
die Clavier ... soll ich es oft
... mit Rücksicht auf die
... zeit wenn es nothwendig ist
zu viel zu kürzen. Mein ... Werk
ist mir leid – aber zu lang ist es ...
... Hochachtung mit ...
Ihr ergebener Ant. Dvořák

Continuation of the letter to Dr. Mandyczewsky

Poster for the first performance in
Prague of the oratorio "St. Ludmila"

On April 19th, 1896, in Olomouc, "St. Ludmila"
was given its fifth performance under the baton
of the composer

In 1901 the National Theatre did a stage performance of "St. Ludmila"

*On June 16th, 1891, an honorary doctor's degree of music was conferred
on Antonín Dvořák by Cambridge University.*

"In Folk Tone". 4 songs, Op. 75; No. 1. "Good-night"

In the short periods between his journeys to England he wrote a number of lyrical works.

The "Rusalka" villa, adapted from an old sheep-farm

A. Dvořák — a passionate pigeon breeder

View of Vysoká

Having bought an old sheep-farm in Vysoká near Příbram in 1883, he turned it into the place where he spent the happiest times of his life.

Střebsko — a small village which he could see from his garden

Pavilion in the garden at Vysoká

The table in the garden

Close to nature and amongst the people, it was at this simple table in the garden that Dvořák wrote some of his most famous works.

November 18th, 1883, was a holiday for all the Czech people: The National Theatre had been completed and was opened that day.

The National Theatre, Prague

Josef Zítek, the architect
of the National Theatre

The auditorium

*It was the first monumental palace or rather shrine that was built in
Prague by the Czech people themselves, not by the ruling class, the
bishops and the aristocrats. The people had paid for it and the artists
gave them their very best ... (Fr. Žákavec).*

Kr. české zemské divadlo v Praze.
Národní divadlo.

V neděli dne 18. listopadu 1883.   Začátek o 12. hodině v poledne.

Otevření Národního divadla.
SLAVNOSTNÍ AKADEMIE.

Program:

SLAVNOSTNÍ PŘEDEHRA
od *Bedřicha Smetany.*

Proslov
od *Jaroslava Vrchlického,* mluví paní *M. Bittnerová.*

HUSITSKÁ.
Slavnostní ouvertura od *Ant. Dvořáka.*
Provede orchestr kr. česk. zem. divadla. Řídí kapelník *M. Anger.*

Slavnostní kantata
od *Karla Bendla.* Slova od *Adolfa Heyduka.*
Přednese pěvecká jednota „*Hlahol*" řízením sbormistra p. *K. Knittla.*

Živý obraz.
Sestavený vrchním režisérem panem *Fr. Kolárem,* provázený básní
J. Vrchlického a hudbou *Z. Fibicha.* Slova pronese p. *J. Seifert.*

Přístup k této akademii mají jen členové sboru pro zřízení Národního divadla, dále ti kdož
v Národním divadle pracovali a zvaní hosté. Lístky k akademii byly zdarma rozeslány
a u divadelní kasy se neprodávají.

Knihtiskárna „Politiky" v Praze. — Nákladem vlastním.

Programme of the inaugural concert with
which the National Theatre was opened

F. A. Schubert, a friend of
Dvořák's, who was the first
director of the National
Theatre

*A. Dvořák wrote the dramatic overture "Husitská" for the ceremonial
opening of the National Theatre. It was conducted by his friend M. Anger.*

Two memorable objects of interest:
The Maleč Castle, home of the librettist M. Červinková-Riegrová

Lužany Castle
(according to Mařák)

Ant. Dvořák visited Maleč Castle several times. It was here that the librettos for "Dimitri" and "The Jacobin" were written. It was at the Lužany Castle that he completed the piano arrangement of the 'cello concerto in B minor, and on another occasion wrote the greater part of his last symphonic poem, "The Hero's Song", Op. 111.

L. Michalek: Antonín Dvořák 1891

Marie Červinková-Riegrová was the author of the libretto

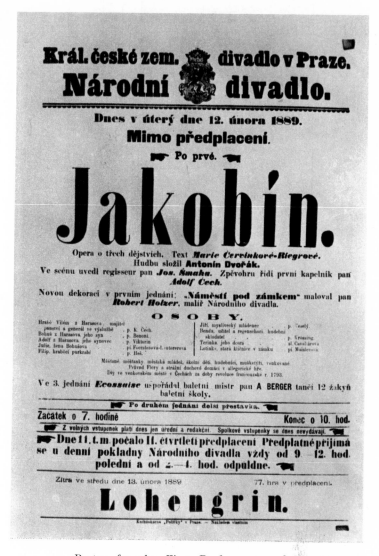

Poster for the First Performance of "The Jacobin"

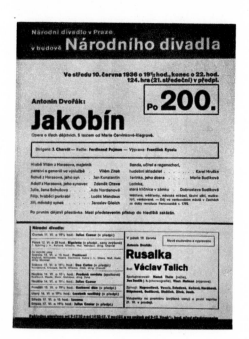

In 1936 "The Jacobin" had its 200th performance at the National Theatre

The opening of the new theatre encouraged Czech composers to greater creative efforts in the field of dramatic music. Dvořák's "The Jacobin" was one of those works produced under this very stimulation.

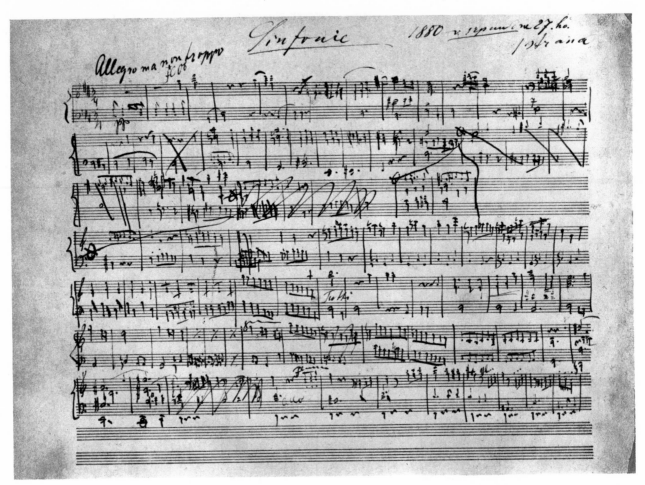

Antonín Dvořák: Sketch for the D major Symphony, which he dedicated to Hans Richter

Title page of the manuscript "Poetic Tone-Pictures"

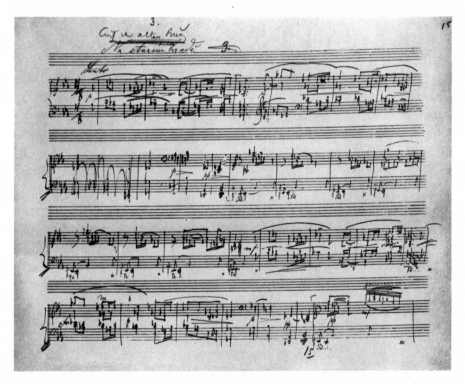

"At the Old Castle", No. 3 of the "Poetic Tone-Pictures"

The "Poetic Tone-Pictures" were a charming expression of repose between the opera "The Jacobin" and the G major Symphony.

Petr Ilyich Tchaikovsky

Tchaikovsky visited Prague twice in 1888 and conducted two concerts there. The two masters formed a profound and close friendship.

<u>18/30</u> Янв. 1889
с. Фроловское

Милый, дорогой, многоува=
жаемый другъ!

Вы не можете себѣ и
представить до чего я
обрадованъ былъ письмомъ
Вашимъ. Мнѣнiе Ваше
объ моей оперѣ мнѣ
особенно цѣнно не
только потому что Вы
великiй художникъ,

но и потому что Вы
правдивый и искреннiй
человѣкъ! Я горжусь,
я счастливъ до послѣдней
степени тѣмъ, что мнѣ
удалось заслужить
слово искренняго со=
=чувствiя именно отъ
Васъ, мой добрый,
многоуважаемый другъ!
Спасибо Вамъ еще
разъ отъ всего сердца...!

A letter from P. I. Tchaikovsky to A. Dvořák

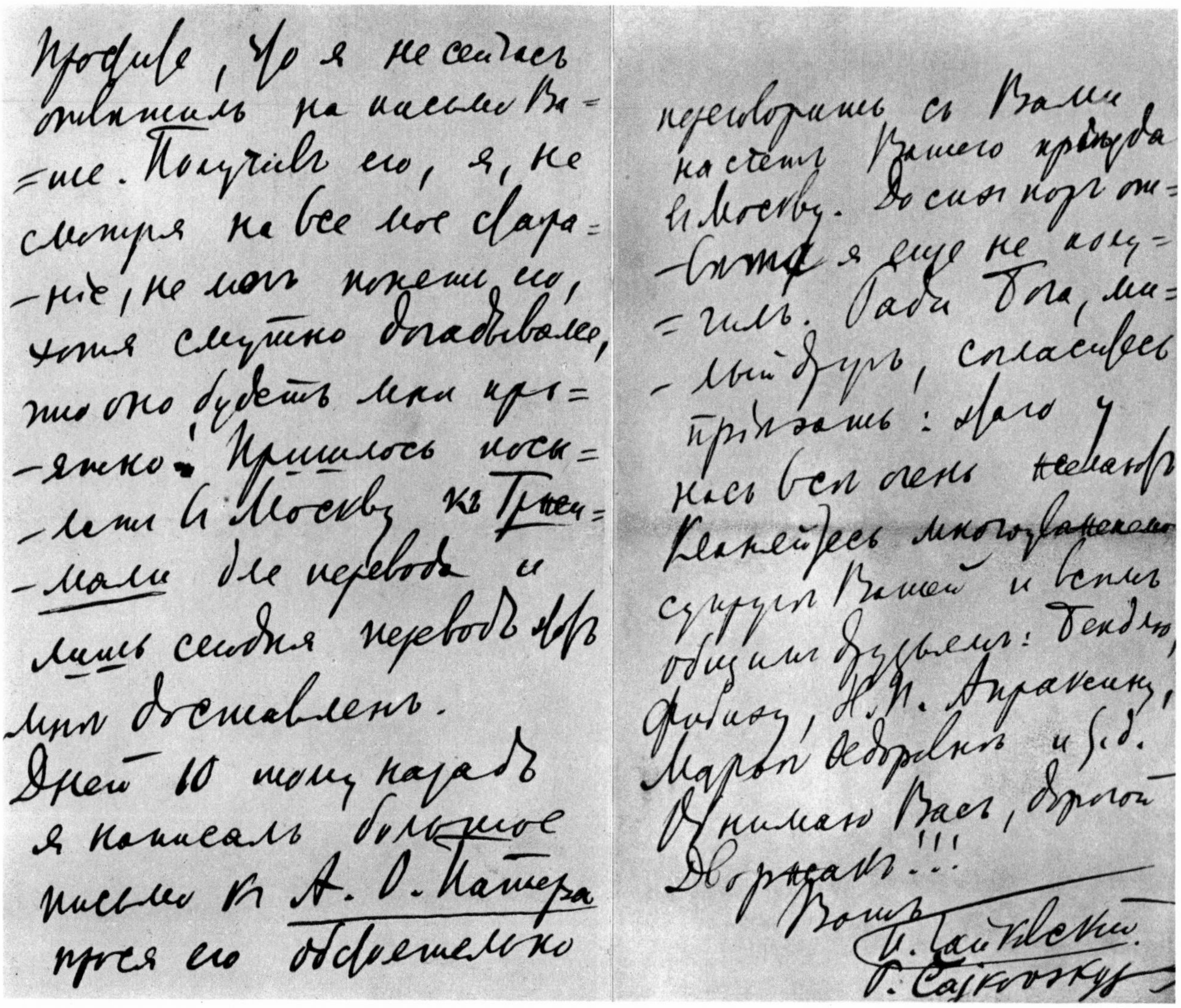

Простите, что я не сейчас
отвечаю на письмо Ва-
=ше. Получив его, я, не
смотря на все мое стара-
-ние, не мог прочесть его,
хотя смутно догадывался,
что оно будет мне при-
-ятно. Пришлось посы-
-лать в Москву к Грже-
-мали для перевода и
лишь сегодня перевод его
мне доставлен.
Дней 10 тому назад
я написал большое
письмо к А. О. Патера
прося его обстоятельно
переговорить с Вами
на счет Вашего приезда
в Москву. До сих пор от-
-вета я еще не полу-
-чил. Ради Бога, ми-
-лый друг, соглашайтесь
приехать: много у
нас все очень желают.
Кланяйтесь многоуважаемой
супруге Вашей и всем
общим друзьям: Бендлю,
Фибиху, Н. П. Апраксину,
Марье Федоровне и т. д.
Обнимаю Вас, дорогой
Дворжак!!!
Ваш
П. Чайковский
P. Čajkovskij

P. I. Tchaikovsky to Dvořák

27 März 1882
Wien

Mein lieber, guter, hoch-
=geschätzter Freund!

Obgleich ist es mir fürch=
terlich schwer deutsch
zu schreiben aber ich
muss doch diese Sausla=
roische Sprache geb=
rauchen um Ihnen
zu sagen dass ich sehr
oft an Ihnen gedacht
habe, dass ich nie ver=
=gessen werde wie Sie

gut und freundlich mich
in Prag empfangen haben.
Ich bin 3½ Wochen in
Paris geblieben (wo
meine Concerte sehr gro=
sen Erfolg gehabt haben)
dann in London wo auch
alles ganz gut war
und jetzt setze ich
zurück nach Russland
und ich nur durchrei=
send in Wien Lieber
Freund, grüssen sie herz=
lich Ihre liebe Frau

Letters from Tchaikovsky to Dvořák

ist sehr gut und besonders
vom Blatt lesen diese
Leute ganz merkwürdig.
Wir haben sehr viel
über Ihnen mit Berger
und andere gesprochen;
man erwartet Ihre
Symphonie mit Ungeduld
Waldek Modriček hat
in demselben Concert
sehr schön gespielt
Herzliche Grüsse an
Bendl, Fibich, Kwardgewold
Modriček junior, Neruda, Čech,
Simer und alle
gute Freunde Auf
Wiedersehen ...!!!

Zemiklin und lassen
die mich noch einmal
sagen dass ich sehr froh
und glücklich bin
dass ich Ihre theure
Freundschaft erworben
habe Im November
hoffe ich, sie wieder
zu sehen. Ich drücke die
Ihnen kräftig die
Hand und
verbleibe Ihr
treuer Freund
P. Tschaikovsky
P. S. Das Orchester in London

On Tchaikovsky's instigation, Dvořák undertook the journey to Moscow
and Petrograd in 1891, in order to conduct several of his works there.

E. Nápravník

V. J. Safonov

The composer Vasil J. Safonov and E. Nápravník were responsible for the production of Dvořák's works in Russia.

The "Dumky" piano trio, the author's arrangement
for four hands

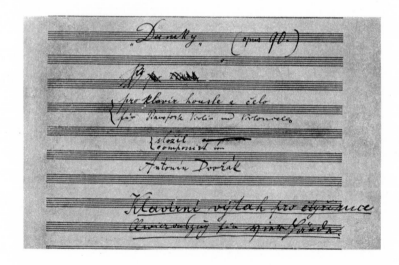

The "Dumky", Op. 90, a six-movement piano trio, is a profound example
of the national character of Dvořák's music.

Manuscript of the Piano Quintet, Op. 77

Dr. Antonín Dvořák 1891

The House of Artists, formerly the Prague Conservatoire

Dr. Josef Tragy, according to the
painting by J. Rolletschek

*Dr. Josef Tragy succeeded in persuading Antonín Dvořák to become
a professor at the famous Prague Conservatoire of Music. His activities
were interrupted by a three year visit to America.*

New York at the end of the 19th century

Jeanette Thurber, founder of the
National Conservatoire of Music in
New York

In 1892 Dvořák accepted the post of director of the National Conserva-
toire of Music in New York. Jeanette Thurber is responsible for the fact
that he spent three years in America.

The ship Saale which took Dvořák to America

J. J. Kovařík, Dvořák's pupil who accompanied his teacher to America

Dvořák's family, shortly after their arrival in the USA

East 17th Street, where Dvořák lived when in New York

Central Park, the scene of his daily walk

Battery Park, from which he could watch the ships which had to take the place of his beloved steam-engines

Programme of a concert given by Dvořák's pupils   Broadway, where Dvořák often used to walk

Madison Square

The great artist was amazed by the new surroundings, he was impressed by his reception and by his success, but homesickness is already apparent in his New World Symphony, written at the beginning of 1893.

Antonín Seidl, conductor of the New York
Philharmonic Orchestra

Carnegie Hall

*Dvořák conducted his first two concerts in the Carnegie Hall on October
21st and on November 17th, 1892. It was here, on December 16th, 1893,
that the first performance was given of the New World Symphony
in E minor, under the baton of A. Seidl.*

First page of the manuscript score of the New World Symphony in E minor

Sketch for the third movement of the New World Symphony score

Dvořák monument at Spillville

DR. DVORAK'S GREAT SYMPHONY.

"From the New World" Heard for the First Time at the Philharmonic Rehearsal.

ABOUT THE SALIENT BEAUTIES.

First Movement the Most Tragic, Second the Most Beautiful, Third the Most Sprightly.

INSPIRED BY INDIAN MUSIC.

The Director of the National Conservatory Adds a Masterpiece to Musical Literature.

MR. SEIDL LEADING THE NEW DVORAK SYMPHONY.

Dr. Antonin Dvorak, the famous Bohemian composer and director of the National Conservatory of Music, dowered American art with a great work yesterday, when his new symphony in E minor, "From the New World," was played at the second Philharmonic rehearsal in Carnegie Music Hall.

The day was an important one in the musical history of America. It witnessed the first public performance of a noble composition.

It saw a large audience of usually tranquil Americans enthusiastic to the point of frenzy over a musical work and applauding like the most excitable "Italianissimi" in the world.

The work was one of heroic proportions. And it was one cast in the art form which such post-musicians as Beethoven, Schubert, Schumann, Mendelssohn, Brahms and many another "glorious one of the earth" has enriched with the most precious outwellings of his musical imagination.

And this new symphony by Dr. Antonin Dvorak is worthy to rank with the best creations of those musicians whom I have just mentioned.

Small wonder that the listeners were enthusiastic. The work appealed to their sense of the æsthetically beautiful by its wealth of tender, pathetic, fiery melody; by its rich harmonic clothing; by its delicate, sonorous, ever varying instrumentation.

And it appealed to the patriotic side of them.

For had not Dr. Dvorak been inspired by the impressions which this country had made upon him? Had he not translated these impressions into sounds, into music? Had they not been assured by the composer himself that the work was written under the direct influence of a serious study of the national music of the North American Indians? Therefore were they not justified in regarding this composition, the first fruits of

HERR ANTONIN DVORAK

Dr. Dvorak's musical genius since his residence in this country, as a distinctly American work of art?

Thus there was every reason for enthusiasm.

Even the orchestra seemed to be transformed by the singular beauty of the symphony. Certainly the members put ever so much better work into it than they had previously exhibited in the preceding part of the programme. Even Mr. Seidl seemed to lose somewhat of his usual impassive air of calm authority as with quick, nervous gestures he communicated his wishes to the Philharmonic Orchestra.

It was essentially a "ladies'" day. The Philharmonic rehearsals always are. But yesterday, in particular, Carnegie Music Hall seemed to contain nothing but the members of the fairer sex.

The downpour of rain could not keep them away. At half-past one there were small groups of enthusiastic admirers of the Philharmonic, of music, of Dr. Dvorak, of Marteau scattered about the great hall, chatting merrily, and, to tell the truth, rather noisily, about a variety of matters—principally private, though that by no means caused them to moderate their voices.

Outside there was a long line of tardy ticket purchasers. Each individual in the row, which stretched down the steps and along Fifty-seventh street, impatiently tried to push forward his immediate predecessor. The others were like the people spoken of by the prophet who would "rush to and fro." And heartily tired of it all they looked long before the flutes gave the first notes of the "Midsummer Night's Dream" overture.

No one seemed quite at ease during the earlier part of the concert. There was an air of excitement pervading every one. People read and reread the analytical notes accompanying the programme. I am sure that the lady next to me must have known by heart that "Dr. Dvorak made a study of Indian and negro melodies and found ther-possessed of characteristics peculiarly their own," That "he identified himself with their spirit, made their essential contents not their formal, external traits, his own," and that he had striven "to reproduce in the present symphony the fundamental characteristics of the melodies which he had found here by means of the specifically musical resources which his inspiration furnished.

At any rate, she studied the remarks with an intensity that was rather awe inspiring.

THE SYMPHONY OPENS.

At last the moment arrives. Mr. Seidl mounts the platform. There is a moment of expectancy. Every eye is on the uplifted baton. It descends. And we are listening at last to Dr. Dvorak's symphony "From the New World."

What do we hear! A sad, tragic unison theme in E minor given out by the 'cellos. Dark, sombre, threatening. The horns throw an instant's flash of color into the scene. Then it is gone and the wood-winds are deepening the feeling of melancholy which the opening passage has created. The strings become more vigorous. The tympani answer sharply, harshly, savagely. Gloom deep as darkest night, created by a long out passage for the contra basses. Slowly the movement begins to be more animated. The wood wind, the strings, everything seems to be upon the qui vive. There is a series of crashing chords, followed by a long roll upon the drum.

Then over a tremolo in the strings the first subject is given out by the horn, the introduction is at an end and the allegro has commenced in real earnest.

What the spirit of Indian music may be I do not know. If this movement which is now going on breathes the genuine native atmosphere then certainly the future of music is in the hands of the red man.

The subject is everywhere. The oboe repeats it, the flute mockingly suggests it, the brass wind thunders it out with savage energy in the midst of a great storm of sound.

And then a series of passages ushers in a delicate, plaintive melody wafted forth by the flute and accompanied by easy, flowing counterpoint. This is followed by a pastoral effect, caused by the clarinet playing a simple, naïve air, above a drone bass. A climax is evidently coming. The strings begin to work up to a crescendo, which suddenly dies away as the flutes enter with a charming, tripping figure that sets your heart beating more rapidly. A murmuring accompaniment, vague and undefined, supports a delightful melody which the 'cellos are singing—and singing very well, it may be remarked en passant.

The development of the themes in this movement is remarkably good. The themes themselves are augmented, diminished, metamorphosed by changing harmonies, varying rhythms and by every device known to musical science—and to Dr. Dvorak, for he has a host of ideas which are not taught in the schools.

Now, for example, does he obtain that rustling murmur in the orchestra that is so eloquent.

We know the combinations of instruments which are taught. We can analyze the responsive discords between the brass and strings; we can say "that was the horn and it was answering the oboe;" we know that the passage we have just heard was a trumpet call, but where does this pervading impression of immensity come from? Is it caused by some hitherto unknown combination of instruments? If it is the sooner Dr. Dvorak allows the score to be printed, so that the secret can become common property, the better for the concertgoer.

But no. It is, as Dr. Dvorak said, the "spirit" of a national music as distinguished from its formal characteristics. And it is that spirit, passed through the imagination of a great poet.

The first movement is brought to an effective close—after a repetition of the principal theme by the horn, followed by a tranquil passage for the strings and a development of the tripping figure which was first heard in the flute and now in the 'cellos—by the trumpet shrieking out the first subject above the entire orchestra, playing fortissimo.

There was something like an ovation at the end of the movement. For several minutes the applause continued, and Anton Seidl was kept busy bowing in response.

The second movement is an adagio, or rather a larghetto in common time, and in the key of D flat. After a few organlike chords given out by the brass and fagotto, calm and simple as a chorale, a melody is sung by the cor anglais above an accompaniment of muted strings. Such an exquisite melody, so sad, so tender so reflective. The strings enter in counterpoint, the flute adds a few notes, pure and tranquil, and after an ascending arpeggio for the clarionet the melody closes in a long sustained chord in the higher registers of the wood wind. The adagio goes on until a rocking figure is commenced by the strings, and below this the 'cellos chant a tender, peaceful air. It is charming. There are some effects of harmony of supreme beauty and piquancy. The cor anglais again enters—this time a little out of tune—a misfortune—and then an entirely novel subject is introduced by the clarionet above a tremolo in the strings. This is well developed, there is a bit of counterpoint between the first violins and flute, and then above a tremolo in the 'cellos, a broad, dignified melody is given out by the violins with great sonority. The oboe enters, the flute answers and then there is a passage—is it in the stringss—that suggests the murmur of human voices. It causes a shiver of expectancy.

But there are no voices. The brass enters above a long roll on the drum. The cor anglais again commences its pathetic melody. The first violins complete it in a hesitating way. The melody is broken, interrupted, unfinished. Again it commences. There is a calm, descending pas-

The journey which A. Dvořák undertook with his family in the summer of 1893 to the Middle West and to Canada. From the book by O. Šourek, "Antonín Dvořák"

Spillville

Dvořák Highway and the house in which he lived

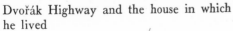

From his Spillville retreat

A. Dvořák spent the summer of 1893 with his Czech countrymen in Spillville, happy to be in the natural surroundings of the countryside; here he wrote the String Quartet in F major, Op. 96, and the Quintet for Strings in E flat major, Op. 97.

The Chicago World Fair, August 1893

J. Popell: The Niagara Falls

On his way home Dvořák visited the Chicago World Fair and took
a trip to the Niagara Falls.

"Czech Day" at the Chicago World Fair

E. V. Nádherný — Chicago: A. Dvořák
conducting at the Chicago World Fair

The streets of Chicago — during the Fair, 1893

*Happy to be amongst his own people, Dvořák took part in "Czech Day"
on August 13th, 1893, at the Fair, and in the Festival Hall conducted
a performance of his overture "My Country"*

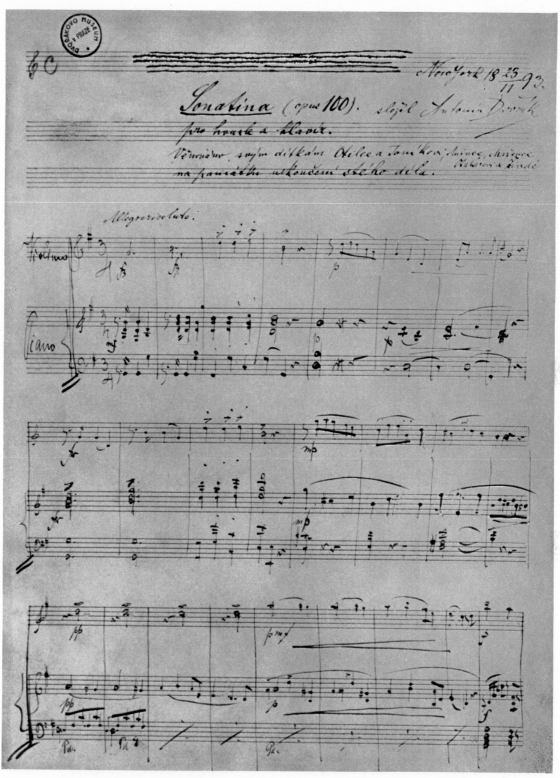

He composed his 100th work in America, the Sonatina for Violin and Piano
He wrote it for his children whom he loved very dearly

Biblical Songs arranged for orchestra

J. Mařatka: Antonín Dvořák

During the final year of Dvořák's stay in America he composed two
famous works, the "Biblical Songs", Op. 102 and the 'cello concerto in
B minor, Op. 104

Gustav Mahler   Richard Strauss

Artur Nikisch   Oskar Nedbal, a pupil of Dvořák's

Famous conductors played his equally famous works in all parts of the world.

Hanuš Wihan, member of the Czech
Quartet, to whom Ant. Dvořák dedicated the 'cello concerto in B minor

The 'cellist Hugo Becker

Ladislav Zelenka, member of the Czech Quartet

*The first interpreters of Dvořák's concerto for 'cello and orchestra in
B minor, Op. 104.*

Romance for Violin and Orchestra —
arranged by A. Dvořák for piano and
dedicated to Fr. Ondříček

František Ondříček

A poster for the concert in honour
of Fr. Ondříček's 50th birthday

Fr. Ondříček was a devoted pioneer of Dvořák's works.

Karel Hoffmann — leader of the
Czech Quartet

Jan Kubelík

J. Herold, of the Czech Quartet

The Herold Quartet — J. Herold,
A. Paleček, O. Vávra, M. Škvor

*The best Czech violinists brought added glory to the name of Dvořák
both at home and abroad.*

The Czech Quartet in its original form: K. Hoffmann, J. Suk,
O. Berger, O. Nedbal

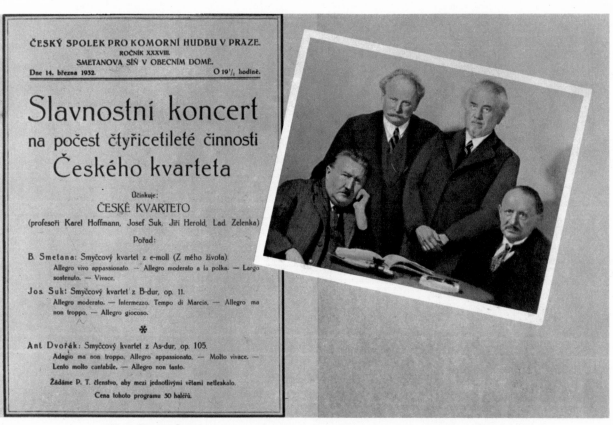

The Czech Quartet as it celebrated its 40th year of activity: J. Suk,
L. Zelenka, J. Herold, K. Hoffmann

*This world-famous quartet was from the first a noble propagator of
Dvořák's works.*

Score of the symphonic poem — "The Wild Dove"

On his return from America Dvořák finished the Quartet in A flat
major, Op. 105, and wrote the Quartet in G major, Op. 106. Then he
once more in 1896 turned to the poems of K. J. Erben "The Bouquet"
and from four of the ballads created the symphonic poems: "The Water
Goblin", "The Noon-day Witch", "The Golden Spinning-Wheel" and
"The Wild Dove".

View of the Moravian town Kroměříž

Dr. E. Kozánek

Leoš Janáček

P. J. Geisler

At the turn of the century Dvořák's works were being greeted with tumultuous applause in all the concert halls of the world. They took particularly deep roots amongst the people of Moravia. This was due to the work of Leoš Janáček, Dr. E. Kozánek, P. J. Geisler, the "Žerotín" Choral Society, the "Moravan", the "Brno Society" and "The Moravian Teacher's Choral Society".

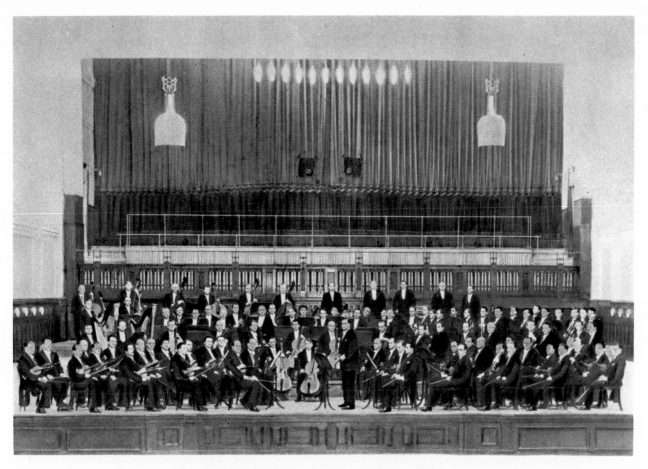

The Czech Philharmonic with Václav Talich

Dr. Boettinger: Josef Suk, Václav Talich, Vítězslav Novák

The Czech Philharmonic from its earliest days was a devoted performer of Dvořák's works.

Hugo Boettinger: Dr. Antonín Dvořák, 1901

Title page of the piano score

Adolf Wenig, author of the libretto of "The Devil and Kate"

A poster for the First Performance of "The Devil and Kate"

During the last few years of his life Dvořák devoted himself entirely to opera.

Edvard Grieg

Dvořák met the famous composer Edvard Grieg during the latter's stay in Prague in 1903. Mutual admiration was the basis of the friendly sympathy which they showed one another on this occasion.

Dr. Antonín Dvořák, 1901

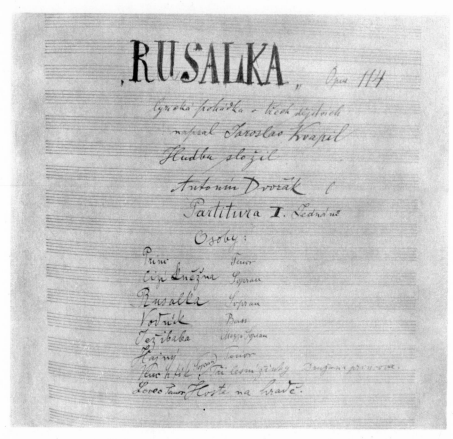

Title page of the score of the opera "Rusalka"

Jaroslav Kvapil, author of the libretto of "Rusalka"

Karel Kovařovic, who conducted its first performance on March 31st, 1901

From the score of the opera "Rusalka"

A. Štrnadel: Ant. Dvořák
(wood-engraving)

Poster for the 600th performance of "Rusalka"
at the National Theatre

*With "Rusalka" he created a fairy-tale opera which **became** world famous.*

The National Museum in Prague

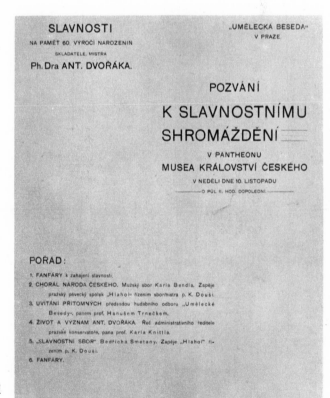

Invitation to the festive gathering held
in honour of Dvořák's 60th birthday

Antonín Dvořák's 60th birthday celebration was treated as a great national jubilee. A festive gathering was held in his honour in the pantheon
of the National Museum.

Overture to the opera "Armida"

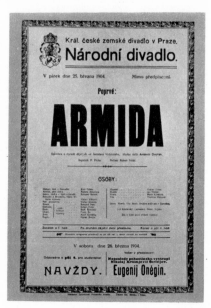

Poster for the First Performance of "Armida"

The opera "Armida" was the last work of this great classic master of Czech music.

V hlubokém žalu podáváme tímto truchlivou zvěst o úmrtí předrahého manžela, otce, tchána a děda, pana

Antonína Dvořáka,

hudebního skladatele, artistického ředitele Pražské konservatoře hudby, rytíře řádu železné koruny III. třídy, majitele čestného znaku pro vědy a umění, doživotního člena panské sněmovny, řádného člena České akademie císaře Františka Josefa I. v Praze, čestného doktora filosofie pražského vysokého učení Karlo-Ferdinandova a university v Cambridgi, čestného člena akademií francouzské, berlínské, srbské, bulharské, společnosti přátel umění ve Vídni, filharmonických spolků v Praze, v New-Yorku, v Budapešti a přemnohých spolků, korporací a jednot českých, čestného setníka c. k. priv. sboru granátníků měšťanské gardy v Praze, majitele zlaté medalie města Paříže atd. atd.,

jenž v neděli 1. dne měsíce května l. 1904 po 12. hodině polední v 63. roce věku svého blaženě v Pánu zesnul.

Pohřeb bude ve čtvrtek 5. dne měsíce května o 3. hodině odpolední z chrámu Páně u sv. Salvatora v Karlově ulici na hřbitov Vyšehradský.

Slavné zádušní mše svaté slouženy budou v sobotu 7. dne měsíce května o 10. hodině dopolední v hlavním farním chrámu Páně u Matky Boží před Týnem.

V PRAZE, dne 2. května 1904.

Josef Suk,	**Anna Dvořáková**	**Otylie** provd. **Suková,**
člen Českého kvartetta,	roz. **Čermáková,**	**Anna** provd. **Sobotková,**
JUDr. **Josef Sobotka,**	manželka.	**Magdalena, Antonín,**
mag. koncipista,		**Otakar** a **Aloisie,**
zeťové.	**Josef Suk,**	děti.
	vnuk.	

Pohřební ústav „Humanitas" F. Bayer v Praze, Karlovo nám. č. 558-II. — Knihtiskárna B. Stýbla v Praze.

On May 1st, 1904, the Czech people was struck with grief and sorrow which spread throughout the world. The genius — the songster of his people — had died.

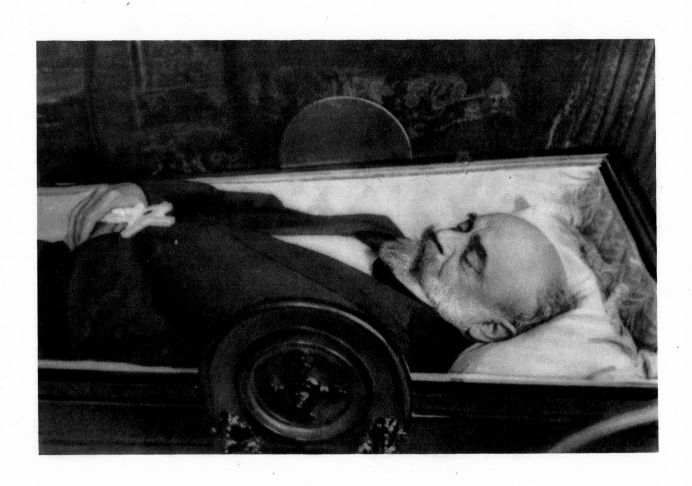

St. Salvator church from where the funeral procession started

His last journey led from the St. Salvator church past the National Theatre, across his beloved Charles Square and up to the ancient Vyše-hrad, where he was laid to rest.

The poet Jaroslav Vrchlický, one of Dvořák's librettists, in the funeral procession (First on the left)

"Requiem" at the National Theatre in the memory of Antonín Dvořák

Dvořák's grave in Vyšehrad

The people and the masters of Czech art and science, all accompanied the national artist on his last journey.

Vítězslav Novák   Rudolf Karel

Josef Suk, Dvořák's son-in-law

Dvořák lives through his works and through the works of the great masters who studied with him: Vítězslav Novák, Rudolf Karel, Oskar Nedbal, Josef Suk.

The poet Jaroslav Vrchlický, one of Dvořák's librettists, in the funeral procession
(First on the left)

"Requiem" at the National Theatre
in the memory of Antonín Dvořák

Dvořák's grave in Vyšehrad

*The people and the masters of Czech art and science, all accompanied the
national artist on his last journey.*

Vítězslav Novák

Rudolf Karel

Josef Suk, Dvořák's son-in-law

Dvořák lives through his works and through the works of the great masters who studied with him: Vítězslav Novák, Rudolf Karel, Oskar Nedbal, Josef Suk.

A poster announcing a cycle of Dvořák operas at the National Theatre for the 30th anniversary of his death, conducted by Otakar Ostrčil

The composer Otakar Jeremiáš

The conductor L. V. Čelanský

Dvořák's legacy has been handed on to the present generation by a number of outstanding conductors.

Otakar Šourek, who is recognized
for his profound analysis of Dvořák's works

Josef Zubatý, Dvořák's first bio-
grapher (Portrait by M. Švabinský)

The conductor Václav Talich

*Musicologists have concentrated much attention on the works of Dvořák,
which, like the works of Smetana, have become the property of the people,
and are part of the national heritage.*

The Michna of Vacínov's villa in Prague, built by K. J. Dientzenhofer, has been converted into a Dvořák Museum

Max Švabinský: Antonín Dvořák

The majority of Dvořák's works have become part of the world repertoire. They have evoked tremendous response in his own country. He was and is still loved by the people for the truly democratic and national character of his music, for the popular style of his great masterpieces. And to-day more than ever before, he is an example to all contemporary Czech art fighting alongside the people for peace and socialism.

The Michna of Vacínov's villa in Prague, built by K. J. Dientzenhofer, has been converted into a Dvořák Museum

Max Švabinský: Antonín Dvořák

The majority of Dvořák's works have become part of the world repertoire. They have evoked tremendous response in his own country. He was and is still loved by the people for the truly democratic and national character of his music, for the popular style of his great masterpieces. And to-day more than ever before, he is an example to all contemporary Czech art fighting alongside the people for peace and socialism.